RACQUETBALL FOR EVERYONE
Technique and Strategy

RACQUETBALL FOR EVERYONE
Technique and Strategy

James Sylvis

Canisius College

Illustrations by Betty Luther

Prentice-Hall, Inc.
Englewood Cliffs, New Jersey   07632

Library of Congress Cataloging in Publication Data

SYLVIS, JAMES.
    Racquetball for everyone.

    Bibliography: p. 172
    Includes index.
    1. Racquetball.   I. Title.
GV1003.34.S95 1985   796.34'3   84–15897
ISBN 0–13–750324–5

Editorial/production supervision and
    interior design: Patricia V. Amoroso
Cover design: Whitman Studio, Inc.
Manufacturing buyer: Harry P. Baisley

Printed in the United States of America

10 9 8 7 6 5 4 3 2 1

ISBN 0-13-750324-5 01

PRENTICE-HALL INTERNATIONAL, INC., London
PRENTICE-HALL OF AUSTRALIA PTY. LIMITED, Sydney
EDITORA PRENTICE-HALL DO BRASIL, LTDA., Rio de Janeiro
PRENTICE-HALL CANADA INC., Toronto
PRENTICE-HALL HISPANOAMERICANA, S.A., Mexico City
PRENTICE-HALL OF INDIA PRIVATE LIMITED, New Delhi
PRENTICE-HALL OF JAPAN, INC., Tokyo
PRENTICE-HALL OF SOUTHEAST ASIA PTE. LTD., Singapore
WHITEHALL BOOKS LIMITED, Wellington, New Zealand

Contents

4   Strategy, or Controlling the Tempo of the Game   85

5   A Different View of the Hinder Rule: Beware of the Wheel   99

6 Problems Encountered by the Former Tennis Player *105*

7 Exercises for Racquetball *112*

Warm-Up *112*
Dynamic Stretching Exercises *113*
Flexibility *115*
Muscular Strength *119*
Development of Stroke Power *125*

8 Officiating as an Art Form *135*

9 The Rules of Racquetball *140*

1982–84 AARA Official Rule Book *140*
The Game *140*
Courts and Equipment *142*
Officiating and Play Regulations *143*
Tournaments *159*
One Wall and Three Wall Rules *162*
Rules for 8 & Under No Bounce *163*
How To Ref When There Is No Ref *163*

Glossary *166*

Bibliography *172*

Index *175*

PREFACE

Over the past ten years racquetball has been one of the fastest growing participant sports in the United States. A study by the A. C. Nielson Company estimated that the number of participants increased by 172 percent from 1976 to 1979. Although this tremendous rate of growth has tapered off, there are still large numbers of individuals beginning to play racquetball. These individuals bring a variety of athletic and sport backgrounds to their involvement in racquetball. *Racquetball for Everyone: Technique and Strategy* offers a unique systematic series of instructional lessons designed to help beginning, intermediate, and advanced players to use their movement abilities as a basis for the acquisition of racquetball skills.

It is generally accepted that individuals learn more readily if they can read about an activity, see it performed, physically attempt it, and then receive feedback on the performance. This is the premise of this text. Chapters 1 and 2 introduce players to the game of racquetball and to the system of instruction used in the practice sessions.

Chapter 3 is a major departure from current racquetball instructional texts. It includes eighteen one-hour practice sessions that can be used by two or more players. Each session is composed of an introduction to the skill; warm-up activities; a task analysis of the skill with drawings and diagrams; a series of progressive practice drills; and a checklist for performance evaluation. The sessions move players from simple eye-hand coordination tasks through advanced overhead shots. Players can progressively move through all sessions or select a specific skill and work on its improvement.

The remainder of the text addresses several problem areas encountered by beginning and advanced players. The format used in the text attempts to mix information related to the performance of racquetball skills with reciprocal teaching methodology. The result is a programmed presentation that can make racquetball truly a game for everyone.

ACKNOWLEDGMENTS

This book is a compendium of knowledge that I have managed to accumulate during my many frustrating losses (mixed with a few glorious victories) in racquetball. My opponents are partly responsible for this book, for they have taught me how to play the game. The theories and skills presented here have been discussed, experimented with, and developed by John Moshides and me throughout many years of friendship. We have spent many hours on the court attempting to develop new methods of performing and teaching various racquetball skills. The true test of any theory is whether it works in practice. Kim Fiedler and Conbow Corporation have given me the opportunity to introduce these methods of teaching at the Boulevard Mall Racquet and Fitness Center in Amherst, New York.

I would also like to thank Tom Haney of the Village Glen Tennis and Fitness Club, for adding his expertise to this endeavor by writing the chapter on exercises for racquetball. For the many illustrations that bring meaning and life to the text I thank Betty Luther.

I dedicate this book to my father. He was a driving force in my early development as an athlete. We devoted many hours to heated discussions of sport skills and strategies. I am sure that my interest in breaking games and skills down into their smallest components comes from those conversations. Last, but not least, I thank my wife Kalat for the times we have had together and my daughters Katie and Kara for the times to come.

INTRODUCTION

My association with Jim Sylvis began about five years ago, when we first met as racquetball competitors. Since our early encounters, we have become good friends and fellow teaching pros and are now involved in a player-coach relationship.

Jim was an all-around athlete who participated mainly in team sports during his formative years. He first discovered racquet sports in 1970 while working on his Ed.D. degree at the State University of New York at Buffalo. Jim first developed his racquet skills playing squash and badminton and then joined the racquetball craze when the industry began to grow in the early 1970s. At this time he completed his doctoral degree and joined the Physical Education Department at Canisius College in Buffalo, New York. At Canisius he has been involved in both the intramural and instructional aspects of racquetball. He has conducted numerous clinics and private lessons, contributed several articles to the *National Racquetball Magazine*, and served as a club program consultant. As a competitor, Jim has consistently finished in the top four of tournaments he has entered and has been ranked as high as fourth in the New York State Seniors Division.

Jim brings this background and his expertise in the methods of teaching to the development of this book. The creation of the task analysis method of racquetball instruction grew from the realization that all players could reach their potential if they had a systematic method of practicing, evaluating, and correcting their skills. For most people, this is much less traumatic and more enjoyable when it is accomplished on their own or with a friend. Thus, the creation of *Racquetball for Everyone: Technique and Strategy.*

I am sure that you will find the content of this innovative book extremely helpful in the development of your racquetball skills. Just keep in mind that the heartbeat of the book is the constant feedback that this style of learning provides. No matter what level of play you may have attained, a continual analysis of your game along the guidelines set out here will help you to maintain progress. Enjoy reading the book and have fun with racquetball!

JOHN MOSHIDES

1981–1982 NEW YORK STATE OPEN CHAMPION, COLLEGE ALL-AMERICAN, 2-TIME JUNIOR REGIONAL CHAMPION

Dr. Jim Sylvis is well known throughout the east coast as an excellent racquetball player and a gentleman on the court. Even more impressive is his reputation as a teacher. His knowledge of the strokes and strategies to be used in racquetball is nonpareil.

In *Racquetball for Everyone: Technique and Strategy,* Dr. Sylvis, a teacher by profession, shows you different methods that he has used to help racquet ball players improve their skills on their own. His easy-to-follow, yet thorough instructions are a must for all racquetball players who sincerely want to upgrade their level of play.

CHARLIE "THE GAR" GARFINKEL

12-TIME NATIONAL RACQUETBALL CHAMPION

1

About the Game

HISTORY

Racquetball has had a very brief history. All the other popular recreational games have their roots in antiquity or in more modern European and Asian sports. Racquetball is unique in that it is an entirely American game. The game had its beginnings in the mind of Joe Sobek of Greenwich, Connecticut. Sobek, a tennis and squash pro in the late 1940s, was looking for a different exercise outlet when he began experimenting with some of the basics of racquetball. He called this original game *paddle racquets*.

Sobek was so enamored of the game that he helped to form the first Paddle Racquets Association to promote it. The sport mushroomed during the early 1950s. It attracted more and more players, and the equipment became more and more refined. Sobek devoted a considerable amount of time to the development of the prototype strung racquet and to the lively ball that is still in use today. By the late 1950s, the game had advanced to a point where there was a call for a national championship. The first national championships were held, appropriately, in Connecticut in 1959. Since the early days in Connecticut the game has become so popular that it is now promoted and monitored by two national racquetball associations.

Racquetball has also moved geographically and socially, from a YMCA in Connecticut to private clubs and exclusive hotels throughout the country. Architecturally the courts have evolved from plaster-walled, enclosed handball courts to courts with walls composed of a variety of materials and containing partial glass viewing areas. Experimentation has even begun on a two-way glass wall that will allow spectators to view the action from all angles while players maintain excellent visual contact with the ball.

With all of this innovation and increased sophistication, the game has remained relatively the same as that conceived by Joe Sobek. It is still played on a court which is twenty feet wide, twenty feet high, and forty feet long, with a back wall that is at least twelve feet high. The lines on the court include (1) a short line halfway between the front and back walls, (2) a service line five feet in front of the short line, (3) two service boxes on either side of this service zone that are used during the serve in doubles, and (4) a receiving line five feet behind the short service line (Figure 1-1). The receiving line is a recent addition that was incorporated to protect the server. The person receiving the serve may not enter into the receiving zone until the ball passes the short line. The receiver may then enter the zone, but neither the racquet nor the receiver's body may pass the imaginary plane of the short line. If the receiver enters this area prematurely, the server gets a point.

Racquetball is a very fast-paced game that can be played by two players (singles), three players (cutthroat), or four players (doubles). It is played to twenty-one points, with only the server scoring. The game begins with the serve. The server drops the ball and hits it on the first bounce so that it goes directly to the front wall. After it hits the front wall, it may hit one side-wall, and then it must pass the short service line on the fly to be in play. If the ball hits more than one sidewall, does not pass the short service line, or hits the back wall on the fly, the server gets one more chance to put the ball legally into play.

Once the ball is in play, the opponent must hit the ball either on the fly or before it bounces twice. After the ball is hit, in order to remain in play it must eventually travel to the front wall while still in the air. This means that the ball can hit any combination of walls (back wall, to side-wall, to front wall, for example) so long as it eventually hits the front wall before it hits the floor. If the server commits a fault, it results in a side-out, and the opponent gains the serve but does not win a point. If the receiver commits a fault, the server gains a point.

The game continues in this fashion, with each player attempting to outthink and outhit the other. Historically, the game has been played in this manner with only a few minor variations. This is a very brief description of how it is played. There are many other rules, regulations, and intricacies of play that the true aficionado should

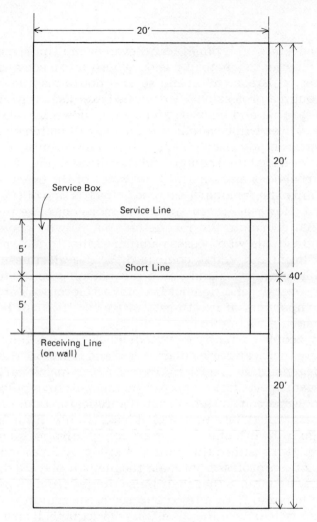

FIGURE 1-1   Dimensions of the court

become familiar with. The complete American Amateur Racquetball Association rules are included in the last chapter.

It is evident that the game is relatively easy to play, is fun, provides a tremendous physical workout, and takes place in an enjoyable and relaxing atmosphere. The combination of these factors, along with the continual innovations in and promotion of the game, is expected to draw over 14 million players to the courts by the mid 1980s—a phenomenal amount of growth in such a short span of time!

BENEFITS

With the advent of the plush, cantilevered, multipurposed racquetball club, playing racquetball has developed into a social event. For a nominal fee, a person can spend several hours playing racquetball; going through a professionally designed exercise program; taking a whirlpool, sauna, and shower; and cooling down by relaxing in the refreshment area while watching a racquetball match or playing the ever-present computerized games. All of these events provide an opportunity for social interaction, and the introduction of co-ed saunas and whirlpools has embellished this aspect of the event.

Certainly the famous "feel good" effect is one of the benefits of racquetball. However, there are other, more objective physiological benefits that accrue to the racquetball player who plays often and against individuals who possess similar skills. In fact, a study conducted by Pipes and Vodak compared the *overall* fitness benefits of fifteen athletic activities and found racquetball second only to swimming as an overall conditioner.[1] Let's take a closer look at some of the specific components of health-related fitness that can be developed through playing racquetball.

Many people participate in racquetball because they feel that it will improve their cardiovascular fitness and therefore their ability to fend off degenerative disorders. In order to improve cardiovascular fitness, most experts feel that a person must attain a pulse rate of 60 percent to 80 percent of his or her theoretical maximum. This rate must be maintained for a period of at least twenty minutes to initiate any change in health status. A good competitive racquetball match puts both players within this range. A study by Pipes monitored the heart rate of ten professional male racquetball players during tournament play and found that their pulse ranged from 78 percent to 92 percent of maximum, or 178 to 195 beats per minute.[2] Allsen used radiotelemetry to determine the effects of racquetball on average club players and found that they reached an average pulse rate of 156 beats per minute during a 30-minute game.[3] Both of these authors concluded that racquetball, if played on a regular basis at this intensity, improves cardiovascular endurance.

Racquetball can also be used to supplement a weight control program. It has been reported that in a highly competitive match the

[1]Thomas V. Pipes and Paul A. Vodak, "A Prescription You Can Fill on the Court," *National Racquetball Magazine,* vol. 8, no. 11 (November 1979), pp. 58–61.

[2]Thomas V. Pipes, "The Racquetball Pro: A Physiological Profile," *Physician and Sports Medicine,* vol. 7, no. 10 (October 1979), pp. 91–94.

[3]P.E. Allsen, "Racquetball Increases Cardiovascular Fitness," *National Racquetball Magazine,* vol. 4, no. 2 (March 1976), p. 39.

players burn approximately eight hundred calories per hour. De-Vries demonstrated that the benefits of exercise continue after the activity has ceased. He found that there was an increase in the resting metabolic rate that lasted up to six hours *after* exercise ceased.[4] This alone could result in a significant weight loss.

Weight loss alone is not the most important measure of the effect of an exercise program. A more meaningful measure is the amount of change in an individual's percentage of body fat. A descriptive study by Pipes found that ten professional racquetball players had an average of 8.1 percent body fat, whereas nonplayers in the same age-group have normal values of from 13 percent to 17 percent.[5] This doesn't necessarily mean that playing racquetball results in this low percentage of body fat; it could be that the lean individual has gravitated to this game or has experienced more success in it.

Pipes also found that the professional racquetball players he profiled were weakest in lower-back and hamstring flexibility and in upper-body strength. He ascribed these weaknesses to lack of a comprehensive training program to develop these components. This lends credence to the argument that racquetball must be supplemented with other forms of exercise in order to round out the overall fitness program

There are many documented benefits that result from playing racquetball. There appear to be other benefits that cannot be categorized and documented, but we know that they exist. The joy of competition, the pleasure of hitting a flat roll-out and of outthinking an opponent, and the delight of recounting these tales over an after-game drink are only a few. The physiological and sociological outcomes are interrelated and enhanced by the atmosphere surrounding the racquetball game. This is a lifetime sport, so you could reap these benefits throughout your lifetime if you continued to participate.

EQUIPMENT

The most essential piece of equipment is the racquet. Racquets come in a variety of geometric shapes, compositions, colors, and prices. The racquet must conform to the following specifications: the head length may be no more than eleven inches and no wider than nine inches; the length of the handle may not exceed seven inches; the total length and width may not be more than twenty-seven inches; and it must include a thong. All commercially produced racquets fall

---

[4]Herbert A. DeVries, *Physiology of Exercise for Physical Education and Athletics* (Dubuque, Iowa: William C. Brown Company, Publishers, 1968), p. 234.

[5]Pipes, "The Racquetball Pro," pp. 91–94.

within these specifications, so these elements are not really critical to racquet selection.

The selection of a racquet should be determined largely by the way it "feels" and looks to you. The feel depends on the grip size, the weight of the racquet, and the tension on the strings. The best way to determine the appropriate feel is to rent and play with various racquets prior to purchasing one. Once you have purchased a racquet, you should play with it awhile before you decide to change its elements or change to another racquet. Ninety-nine percent of the time it isn't the racquet that is causing you to lose; it is the quality of your opponents play and your own shortcomings.

There is a variety of racquetballs on the market, and they too come in a multitude of colors. There are specifications governing the amount of bounce required, but anyone who has played the game knows that there are both lively balls and dead balls produced by different manufacturers, sometimes by the same manufacturer, and sometimes included in the same can! Ball selection for the more competitive players should be based upon the recommendations of the local and national associations governing play. Since there are differences in the way in which the balls play, it is essential to practice with *the* ball that is going to be used in a given tournament or league.

Another essential piece of equipment is the eyeguard. As racquet sports have gained in popularity there has been a parallel increase in the number of eye injuries. The severity of these injuries can range from total loss of vision to slight discoloration. National racquetball associations have made the wearing of eyeguards mandatory in any sanctioned tournaments. This ruling not only protects the eyes, but it could also give a player the courage to look at an opponent during play, thereby improving anticipation and total court sense.

The last critical piece of equipment that effects play is shoes. There are several companies producing racquetball shoes specifically designed for the stresses and strains inherent in the game. These shoes hold up much better over a longer period of time than shoes that have been designed for another purpose or a different sport. Comfort, looks, and durability should guide your selection.

There are several other nonessential items that you can buy to make you feel better about being seen on the court. These include warm-up suits, playing outfits, special socks, gloves, wristbands, headbands, bags, racquet covers, ball pressurizers, and jewelry. Some of these items have utilitarian value, but none (excluding the glove) can improve the play. If you do purchase most of these items you may feel that you at least look like a racquetball player, even in defeat!

2

How to Use the Book

The purpose of using a task style format in an instructional manual is twofold. First, it provides more than a mere description of the skills needed to play. Each session includes a critical analysis of a skill and a series of on-court drills to improve that skill. Second, it involves more of a player's senses in the learning process. You will read, see, and critically analyze your performance of the skills. Herein lies the secret to success. The person who thoroughly understands an activity can more easily modify a skill and adapt it to his or her individual style of play.

The following series of lessons has been designed for a variety of players. The sessions follow a progressive pattern of skill development and evaluation. A prospective player could start at the first session and progress consecutively through all the sessions or begin at an intermediate or advanced level and selectively work on weak skill areas. Chapter 3 covers the racquetball skill spectrum from the uncoordinated beginner, through the player who can't seem to improve his or her game, to the advanced player who would like to hone his or her game skills.

Each session has been designed to fit into a one-hour time frame. For each one-hour period there is a schedule of activities that includes the following sections when applicable:

1. Introduction to the task, explaining its importance to play
2. On-court warm-up (Chapter 7 includes pregame and postgame warm-up and cool-down activities.)

3. On-court organization for the session
4. Explanation of the rules related to the aspect of play being discussed
5. Task practice schedule
6. Evaluation sheet
7. Techniques for correcting common errors

Each session also contains diagrams and drawings that highlight the critical aspects of the activities.

Now that you have read the introductory materials and have some idea of the way in which the sessions work, it is time to get started. For each of the following lessons it is suggested that you read the entire session *prior* to getting on the court. Go through a precourt warm-up (Chapter 7), enter the court and proceed through the tasks listed for the session, evaluate each other's performances, and move on to the next series of tasks when comfortable.

Do not spend an inordinate amount of time on any of the tasks that seem to be particularly difficult for you. It is better to move on and to come back to the more difficult skills later, attempting to improve your performance at that time.

If you find that you are having difficulty getting the "feel" of a particular skill, it might be a good idea to take your evaluation sheet and observe and evaluate an advanced player performing the given skill. A combination of knowledgeable critical analysis, mental practice, and physical practice should help to improve your skills.

You may find that these structured one-hour sessions are not your idea of fun! If this is the case, devote part of the hour to the drills (about ten to fifteen minutes) and the remainder of the time to playing a regulation game. During the games, try to incorporate new skills as the occasions arise. *Remember above all else, the sessions are supposed to be fun!*

3

Practice Sessions

Most motor-learning experts agree that, to improve performance of a given skill, a person must first develop an idea, or mental picture, of the whole movement about to be attempted. Once there is a general understanding of the parameters of the skill, a player can efficiently evaluate and alter performance and thereby enhance the chances of success.

As you go through the following practice sessions, it is critically important that you develop a mental picture of the effective performance of each skill. To help you form this picture, each skill has been broken down into its components. Successful acquisition of each skill depends upon your knowing the function of the following interrelated aspects of performance:

1. Grip
2. Stance or footwork
3. Backswing
4. Racquet path or movement
5. Focal point
6. Contact point
7. Body movement during the stroke
8. Wrist snap
9. Follow-through

You can evaluate your performance of each stroke by determining the effect it has had on the ball. If the effect is poor, the problem exists in one or more of the nine interrelated components of the stroke. Players who have a thorough understanding of each stroke will have little difficulty finding where the problem lies and eventually correcting their mistakes.

SESSION 1   Introduction to Court Movement
(Eye-Hand Coordination)

A. Value of the Task

To play racquetball successfully you must be able to get to the ball, and once there, to hit it! Herein lies the problem with most beginners. They have poor basic running skills and poor eye-hand coordination. These problems are magnified when they attempt to move around in a twenty-foot by forty-foot area and try to hit a wildly bouncing object. The ability to do this is *not* inherited, it is developed. The following drills are designed to improve these capacities.

B. Task Practice 1: Court Movement (5 to 7 minutes)

1. *Star Drill.* Start facing the center of the front wall. Hold your racquet in your dominant hand as you run from number to number (Figure 3-1). Keep your eyes focused on the front wall and attempt to use peripheral vision and "feel" to locate the sidewalls and back walls as you move. Remember that you are simulating a game situation, so try to watch the ball. When you reach each point (number) of the star, try to set up and perform a forehand or backhand stroke (see session 2). You will find that much of this running involves pivoting, shuffle steps, and galloping.

2. *Ceiling Ball Footwork Drill.* Start in the center of the back wall, facing the front wall, with your racquet in hand. Run forward to the center of the short service line; pivot and move to the right backhand corner; pivot and return to the center near the short service line; pivot and go to the deep left corner; return to the center of the short service line and then back to the original starting position (Figure 3-2).

C. Task Practice 2

1. *Eye-Hand Coordination Drills without a Racquet*
   a. Toss a ball into the air at about three-quarters of court height. Attempt to catch it. Repeat five times with each hand.
   b. Toss a ball into the air, turn around, and attempt to catch it before it bounces. Repeat five times with each hand.
   c. Bounce the ball on the floor and catch it. Repeat five times with each hand.

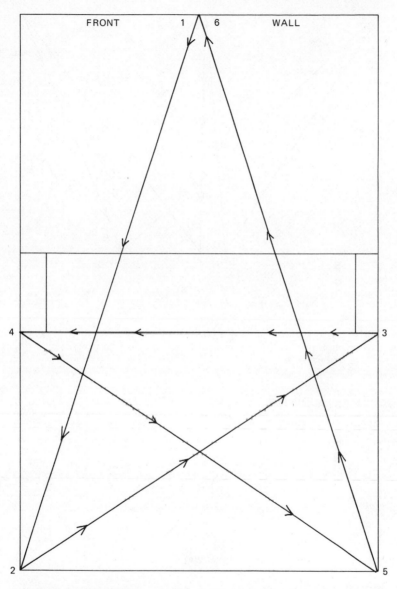

FIGURE 3-1   Star drill

    d. Stand about fifteen feet from the sidewall. Bounce the ball off of the sidewall, and try to catch it on the first bounce. Repeat five times with each hand.

2. *Eye-Hand Coordination Drills with a Racquet*

    a. Hold your racquet at waist height with the face up. Bounce the ball on the racquet as many times as you can.

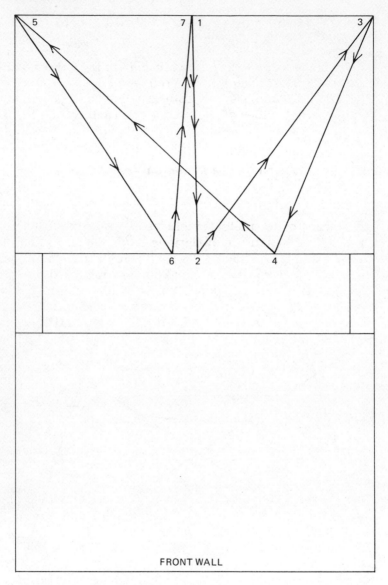

FIGURE 3-2 Ceiling ball footwork drill

b. From the same position, bounce the ball on the racquet, alternating from front side to back side of racquet face.
c. If you can accomplish the first two tasks rather easily, attempt to bounce the ball on the face of the racquet, then the side of the frame, and then the back of the racquet face.
d. Stand fifteen feet from the sidewall and facing it. Attempt

to hit the ball to the sidewall (easily) using a forehand stroke. Catch the ball as it rebounds. Repeat five to ten times.

e. From the same position, hit the ball to the sidewall and try to rally it continuously to yourself.

f. From the same position, hit the ball to the sidewall and try to alternate sides of the racquet on each return stroke.

SESSION 2 *Fundamental Forehand and Backhand Strokes*

A. Value of the Task

The game of racquetball includes several different stroking patterns, all of which are variations of the basic forehand and backhand strokes. Although there are similarities between racquetball and other racquet sport skills, the racquetball stroking pattern is completely unique. Therefore the majority of your practice time should be devoted to the development of fundamentally correct and *consistent* forehand and backhand strokes.

B. On-Court Warm-Up
1. Star Drill (see session 1)
2. Ceiling Ball Footwork Drill (see session 1)

C. Court Organization

Two people should be on the court with racquets. One person stands one foot behind the short service line on the left, and the other person stands in the same position on the right. The person on the right hits forehands, and the one on the left, backhands (assuming both are right-handed) (Figure 3-3).

D. Task Practice
1. Read the sections on mechanics for this session which explain how to hit each stroke. Study the pictures and simulate the swing without a ball.
2. Each person hits fifteen forehands and then switches sides and hits fifteen backhands. For each stroke, you drop the ball in front of you and hit it to the front wall. As it rebounds catch it and repeat. Do not continuously volley the ball.
3. Following this short drill, evaluate each other's forehands and backhands, using the checklist provided at the end of this session.
4. You should end the practice session by testing yourself on the strokes. Attempt to volley the ball continuously to the front wall from behind the short service line. Only legal hits count. Your score is the total number of continuous hits.

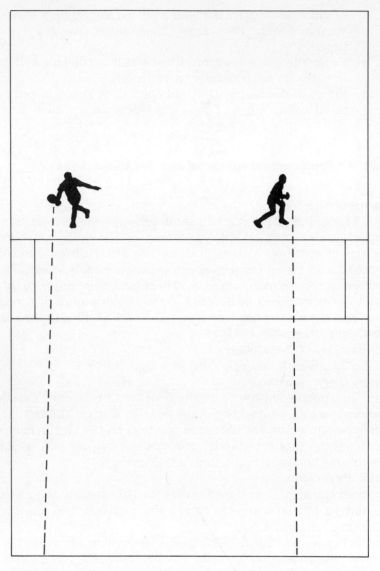

FIGURE 3-3   Forehand and backhand warm-up drill

E. Mechanics of the Task: Forehand Stroke (Figures 3-4—3-8)
  1. *Grip.* The "V" formed by the thumb and index finger should be on the top of the racquet handle.
  2. *Stance.* Face the sidewall, feet a comfortable distance apart.
  3. *Backswing.* The racquet should be very high, elbow at shoulder height, forearm at ninety-degree angle to upper arm.
  4. *Wrist Cock.* This should be toward your head, racquet parallel to the sidewall.

FIGURE 3-4   The forehand grip

FIGURE 3-5   The backswing

FIGURE 3-6   Initiation of the swing

5. *Eye Focus.* Keep your eyes on the ball at all times.
6. *Body and Racquet Movement.* As the racquet begins to move, you step forward with the front foot, and your weight begins to transfer from the back to the front foot. The racquet path should follow a semicircle from the high backswing to the contact point, which is even with your front knee. The racquet

FIGURE 3-7   Straight-arm position at the contact point

FIGURE 3-8 The follow-through

arm should remain bent until the contact point, when it should be brought into a straight position.

7. *Contact Point.* This falls between your knee and ankle and in front of your lead foot after you have taken your step. You may begin with a waist-high contact point, and, as you feel comfortable with your swing, begin to drop it to the more desirable low point.

8. *Wrist Involvement.* At contact, the wrist should snap across your body toward the opposite wall.

9. *Follow-through.* The swing is finished when you have pivoted on your back foot, and your shoulders and hips have turned to squarely face the front wall.

F. Common Errors on the Forehand

1. Swing and miss. *Correction:* Eyes watch the ball fly into the racquet face.

2. Ball goes up toward the ceiling after being hit. *Correction:* Keep the palm of your hand and the racquet face moving toward the front wall. Don't allow the racquet face to slice up toward the ceiling. Check your grip.

3. Ball goes into the floor. *Correction:* Same as in no. 2, because you are rolling your wrist and the palm of your hand over, and the racquet is facing the floor at contact.

4. Ball goes to the left (right-handed player). *Correction:* Move the contact point back in your stance, and slow the wrist action. You are contacting the ball in front of the lead foot or you are breaking the wrist too soon.

5. Ball goes to the right (right-handed player). *Correction:* Move

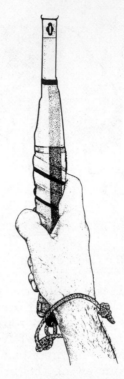

FIGURE 3-9   The backhand grip

the contact point up toward the center of your stance, and break the wrist sooner. You are contacting the ball behind the center of your stance, or you are breaking the wrist after you have contacted the ball.

G. Mechanics of the Task: Backhand Stroke (Figures 3-9–3-14)[6]

1. *Grip.* The "V" formed by the thumb and index finger should be on the first bevel on the left of the racquet handle (right-handed player).
2. *Stance.* Face sidewall, feet a comfortable distance apart.
3. *Backswing.* The arm is bent, and the racquet is held as high as your back shoulder. This will turn your hips toward the back wall.
4. *Wrist Cock.* This is toward your head, racquet parallel to the sidewall.
5. *Eye Focus.* Always keep your eyes on the ball.
6. *Body and Racquet Movement.* As the racquet begins to move,

---

[6]Based upon a series of photographs from Charles Brumfield, "Inside the Master's Mind," *National Racquetball Magazine*, vol. 7, no. 6 (June 1979), pp. 28–32.

FIGURE 3-10 The stance and the beginning of the backswing

you step foreward with your front foot, and your weight shifts from the back to the front foot. The racquet path should resemble a semicircle from the high backswing to the contact point, which is even with the inside of your lead foot. Racquet arm remains bent until contact, and then is brought into a straight position. *At contact, your racquet arm should be in line with your lead shoulder.*

7. *Contact Point.* This falls *behind* your lead foot, between the knee and the ankle.

8. *Follow-through.* At contact, the wrist should snap toward the opposite wall, and the weight should shift to the front foot as the hips and shoulders turn squarely to the front wall.

H. Common Errors on the Backhand

1. Missing the ball. *Correction:* Eyes watch the ball through contact.

2. Ball goes up after contact. *Correction:* Keep the back of the hand heading toward the front wall on contact. Check your grip and your contact point.

3. Ball goes into the floor. *Correction:* Same as no. 2. You may be

FIGURE 3-11 The high backswing and the hip turn

rolling your wrist over at contact (back of your hand is facing the floor). Check your grip and the contact point, which could be too far back in your stance.

4. No power, or you are pushing the ball. *Correction:* Make sure you are snapping the wrist at contact. Check to see if the arm and racquet are in line with your shoulder at the contact point. If the elbow is leading or in front of this line at contact, you will push the ball.

5. Ball goes to the right (right-handed player). *Correction:* Move the contact point back to the inside of the lead foot and break the wrist at contact. Contact point is in front of the lead foot or the wrist is breaking too soon.

6. Ball goes to the left (right-handed player). *Correction:* Move

FIGURE 3-12   Initiation of the swing

the contact point toward the front foot and break the wrist sooner. Contact point is behind the middle of your stance or the wrist is breaking after you hit the ball.

I. Evaluation Checklist   YES   NO

 1. *Forehand Stroke*
   a. Uses appropriate grip
   b. Faces the sidewall
   c. Has a high backswing
   d. Starts swing from the high backswing moving it directly to the ball with arm not dropping to straight position from the backswing
   e. Makes sure arm reaches straight position at contact, not before
   f. Makes sure wrist explodes at contact and goes across the body

FIGURE 3-13 The middle of the swing, with weight on front foot

FIGURE 3-14 Straight-arm position in line with the front shoulder at the point of contact

2. *Backhand Stroke*   <u>YES</u>   <u>NO</u>
   a. Uses appropriate grip
   b. Faces the sidewall
   c. Uses high backswing, with hips turned to back wall
   d. Starts swing from the high backswing moving it directly to the ball
   e. Makes sure arm reaches straight position at contact, not before
   f. Makes sure arm and racquet at contact are in a straight line with the front shoulder
   g. Finds contact point behind the lead foot
   h. Makes sure wrist explodes at contact, turning the hips and shoulders squarely to the front wall
3. Continuous volley score _____ Date _____

SESSION 3   Hitting a Moving Object—Front-Wall Shot

A. Value of the Task

You have now developed the mechanics of the two fundamental strokes—forehand and backhand. The secret of playing winning racquetball is to hit these strokes correctly, consistently, and accurately. This is fairly easy to do in a stationary position. Unfortunately the only time you will be able to hit a stationary stroke is during the serve. Most of the time you must be able to move to a position on the court that allows you to utilize these basic strokes. This session will improve your ability to do this and therefore make you more consistent.

B. On-Court Warm-Up

1. *Step-and-Stroke Drill.* Two people should be on the court with racquets. Face the front wall, with one person standing behind the other in the center of the court. Simulate the forehand stroke by taking a short step with the right foot and a long step diagonally with the left foot toward the right front corner as you perform the stroke. Repeat five times. Simulate the backhand stroke by taking a short step with the left foot and a long diagonal step with the right foot toward the left front corner as you stroke. Repeat five times. Alternate simulated forehands and backhands five times, always returning to the center of the court.
2. Review session 2 mechanics and then hit ten forehands and ten backhands.

C. Court Organization

The person performing the stroke stands in the center court area, and the person throwing the ball stands behind the short service line on the hitter's backhand side.

D. Task Practice

1. The person who is hitting stands in the center court position, facing the front wall. The thrower stands on the backhand side (Figure 3-15).

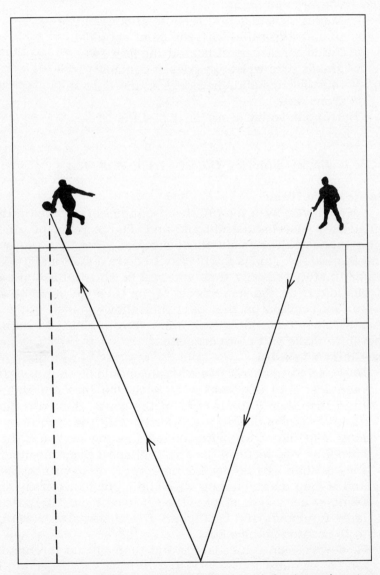

FIGURE 3-15   Hitting a moving ball (thrown) that is coming at you

2. The thrower throws the ball underhand toward the center of the front wall, about head high. The first five throws should be to the hitter's forehand side.

• 3. Get into position to hit (this is called *anticipation*). As the ball *leaves* the thrower's hand, begin to move into a forehand stroking position. Turn and face the appropriate sidewall, and run to a position on the court *behind* the flight of the ball that will allow you to contact the ball in *front* of your body after it has bounced.

4. When you feel you are in the correct position to hit the ball, plant your back foot and get your racquet into a high backswing position. Allow the ball to approach you so that when you make contact it is in front of you and *waist high or lower.*

5. Hit the ball, using the correct stroking pattern, and then return to the center-court position.

6. Follow the same procedures for the backhand stroke. The thrower is now on the forehand side of the hitter.

7. Hit five forehands, five backhands, and ten alternating shots (Figure 3-16).

   NOTE: If you are continually hitting overhead strokes, or if after hitting the ball, it travels to the sidewall or bounces high off the front wall, the problem is that you are not getting into the correct position on the court to hit the ball. You are probably not moving back and away from the ball. Instead you are moving toward the front wall or directly sideward (parallel to the front wall), or you are standing frozen in position as the ball approaches. To eliminate this problem and to set yourself in the proper position for hitting the correct forehand or backhand stroke, try the following drill.

   Take the ball and stand in the center of the court near the short service line. Throw the ball to a point about head high on the front wall. As the ball hits the front wall, turn and face the appropriate sidewall (forehand/backhand) and slide backward until you are in a position to reach *forward* and catch the ball. You should catch the ball at about waist to knee height and close to the leg nearer the front wall. Catch the ball at the point where you will contact it during actual play. To determine how far back you should slide before you are in position for the stroke, you must ascertain the point at which the ball peaks in its flight after it has bounced. Once the ball has peaked, it will begin to drop into the hitting zone (see Figure 3-17). If you slide backward and position yourself at a distance of two to three yards from the point at which the ball peaks, your contact point will be somewhere between your ankle and waist. After you have attempted to throw and catch, and you

FIGURE 3-16 Hitting a moving ball (thrown) with a backhand stroke

feel comfortable with your court positioning and movement, try hitting the ball instead of catching it. When you feel comfortable with this drill, have the other player throw the ball off the front wall and complete the tasks listed.

E. Evaluation Checklist   YES   NO

1. Begins to move as ball leaves thrower's hand

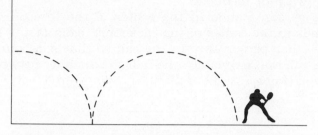

FIGURE 3-17 The ball can be contacted anywhere along the arc following the bounce. The player tries to get to a position behind the peak of the bounce, so that the ball can be contacted at its lowest point.

2. Faces sideways to appripriate wall   <u>YES   NO</u>
3. Moves to a position behind the *low* contact point (If hitting the ball waist high or higher, the player must move back to allow the ball to drop.)
4. Assumes a good high backswing—quickly
5. Plants the back foot—is not moving and hitting at the same time
6. Performs a good stroke and follow-through as evaluated in session 2

SESSION 4   *Hitting a Moving Object—Side Wallshot*

A. Value of the Task

The most frustrating part of racquetball for most beginning players centers around the balls rebounding off different walls at various angles. Getting into position to hit after the ball has struck one, two, or three walls is essential to performing a correct and consistent stroke. The ability is also critical to returning a serve that has struck one sidewall—the bane of most beginners. The next series of tasks will help you to master this problem.

B. On-Court Warm-Up

Drop-and-Hit Drill. One person is on the backhand side and one on the forehand side. Throw an underhand ball to the *sidewall* so that it rebounds to a position slightly in front of you. After it has bounced once, you should hit the appropriate stroke, and then catch the ball as it rebounds off the front wall. Hit ten forehands, switch sides, and hit ten backhands.

C. Task Practice: Taking the Ball off the Sidewall
Task 1 (without racquets)
1. One person stands in the center of the forecourt, and one stands in the center of the backcourt, each *facing* the other.
2. The other person throws the ball so that it rebounds off the sidewall approximately one-half the distance between the two of you (Figure 3-18).

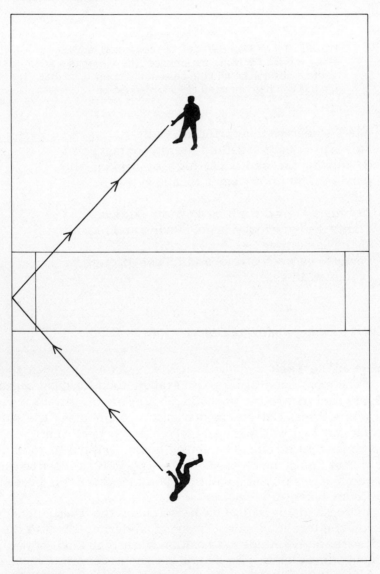

FIGURE 3-18 Getting into position to hit a ball coming off the sidewall

3. When the ball *leaves* the thrower's hand, you move into a simulated forehand position (turn, face the sidewall, and shuffle into position behind the flight of the ball so that you have to reach to catch it). Assume a high backswing position, and then reach out and catch the ball in front of your body with

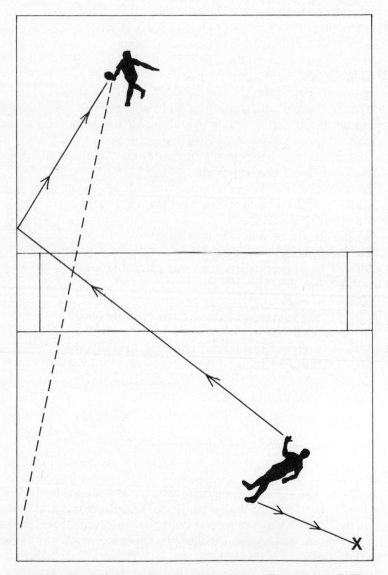

FIGURE 3-19 Hitting a ball coming at you off the sidewall. The thrower's safety depends on a quick movement to the corner following the throw, and on eyeguards.

your racquet hand. This is where you would *hit* the ball if it rebounded off the sidewall.

4. The receiver should return the ball by throwing to your forehand side. Repeat five times.
5. Perform the same task to the backhand side. Repeat five times.

Helpful Hint for Task 1

The ball will always rebound off a wall at the same angle at which it goes into the wall (law of physics). Anticipate! Don't run after the ball. *Don't meet it!* Run to a place where you have anticipated it will come, and *let it come to you!*

Task 2 (with racquets) BOTH PLAYERS SHOULD WEAR EYEGUARDS!

1. Stand in the same positions as you did for task 1.
2. Throw the ball off the *sidewall* to the hitter's forehand side.
3. Immediately *after throwing the ball, move* to the backhand corner of the front wall (Figure 3-19).
4. The hitter will set up and *lightly* hit a forehand stroke as the ball comes off the sidewall.
5. Repeat five times forehand, five times backhand, and five times alternating strokes, and then switch.

D. Evaluation Checklist   YES   NO

1. Begins to move when ball is thrown
2. Faces appropriate sidewall
3. Moves in correct direction (usually *back* and *away* from not toward, the ball)
4. Holds racquet high in backswing
5. Plants rear foot and strokes correctly (not moving while hitting)
6. Makes correct contact point—low and in the area of the lead foot
7. Takes a step, hits the ball, and finishes with a good follow-through

SESSION 5   *Taking the Ball off the Back Wall*

A. Value of the Task

There are actually two different back-wall shots. In the first, the ball hits the front wall, the floor, and the back wall. A player must then hit the ball before it bounces a second time. The second hits the front wall, goes directly to the back wall, and then hits the floor, after which it must be hit. The fundamentals are the same in each shot. The stroke used is the basic forehand or backhand. The only differences are in the visual tracking of the ball and in getting into position to hit. If you can accomplish these two things, these shots become setups, and you should score a point on the next stroke.

B. On-Court Warm-Up

1. *Ceiling Ball Footwork Drill* (see session 1)
2. *Drop-and-Hit Drill.* Stand deep in the court—about five feet from the back wall. Throw the ball off the back wall at about waist height, so that it rebounds and passes in front of you. As the ball passes the center of your body, attempt to hit it to the front wall. Catch the rebound. Repeat ten times. Switch sides, and perform the same task on the backhand side.

C. Task Practice

1. *Task 1: Taking the Ball off the Back Wall—Forehand.* (Players should wear eyeguards during all sessions.)
   a. Both players stand in the backcourt area. The hitter stands about seven feet from the back wall, in a forehand stroking position. The thrower stands on the forehand side, about six feet from the back wall.
   b. The other player throws the ball underhand to the back wall, about two feet above head height. The ball should rebound off the back wall and travel along your forehand side on its way toward the front wall (Figure 3-20 illustrates the backhand drill).
   c. Concentrate on watching the ball as it passes from your back to your front shoulder. Then *catch* the ball with the hand closest to the front wall. Attempt to get a feel for the ball passing to the front part of your body, as this is where the ball should be contacted for an effective back-wall shot. When the ball passes from the back to the front of your body, it should be about *chin high.* If it is not in this position, you should shuffle either forward or backward to assure the correct hitting location. Repeat until you feel comfortable.
   d. Remain in the same positions. This time, as the ball passes to the front, you should hit a forehand stroke to the front wall. Repeat ten times.
      (1) As the ball leaves the thrower's hand, immediately assume a high backswing.
      (2) The ball will be traveling on a different plane from the swing. The ball will be coming from a high to a low position, and the swing will be moving more in a back-to-front plane. The swing must *intersect* the ball somewhere around the level of the front knee. If you swing on the same plane that the ball is traveling, you will hit an overhead type of stroke.
   e. Stand in the center-court area facing the front wall. The

FIGURE 3-20 Getting into position to hit the ball coming off the back wall

other player stands near the short service area on the *back-hand* side. This player hits an underhand stroke to the front wall so that it rebounds, strikes the floor, and hits the back wall. As the ball leaves the racquet, turn and face the forehand wall, get the racquet up into the backswing posi-tion, and move to the anticipated contact point. When the ball passes in front of you, hit a forehand stroke (Figure 3-21).

2. *Evaluation Checklist for Task 1* <u>YES</u> <u>NO</u>
   a. Begins to move to hitting position as ball leaves opponent's racquet
   b. Attains a high backswing immediately

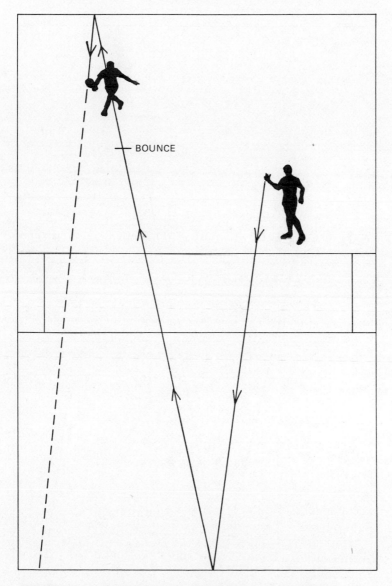

BOUNCE

FIGURE 3-21 Taking the ball off the back wall—forehand

   c. Positions so that ball passes from back to   <u>YES</u>   NO
      front at about chin level
   d. Focuses eyes on the ball throughout
   e. Plants back foot prior to initiation of swing
   f. Makes sure racquet path is on a different
     plane from path of the ball

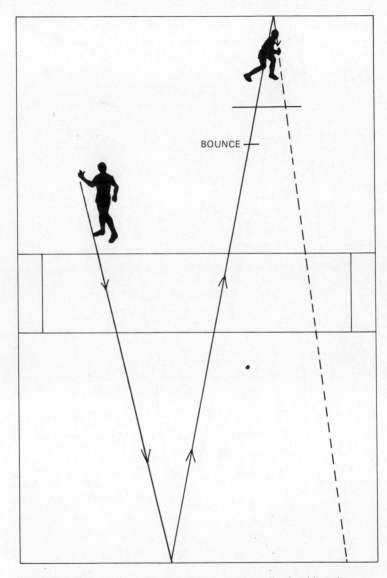

FIGURE 3-22   Taking the ball off the back wall—backhand

g. Contacts the ball in front of the body, near   YES   NO
the front foot (*Critical!*)

h. Finishes stroke with a good follow-through

3. *Task 2: Taking the Ball off the Back Wall—Backhand*

a. The procedures are exactly the same as those used for the forehand back-wall shot except that you hit from the backhand side.

b. The person throwing the ball or setting up the ball by hitting it is now on the opposite side from that suggested in the forehand drills (Figure 3-22).

SESSION 6   Service and Receiving the Serve

A. Value of the Task

You can only score points when you serve; therefore the serve should be an offensive shot used to put your opponent at a disadvantage. There are four basic serves, but this session will only cover the drive and the half-lob serves. The "Z" and lob serves will be explained in a later session. In order to keep the rally going and to win the serve, the person receiving the serve must be able to move and hit the ball back to the front wall. This series of tasks should help both server and receiver.

B. Service Rules

Prior to this practice session you should read the rules on serving, which are included in the chapter on rules (see pp. 146–51).

C. Task Practice

Task 1: The Drive serve—receiver moves and catches the ball

1. *Court organization.* One person is in the center of the service area with a racquet and a ball. The other person is in the receiving position, which is one arm's length from the back wall and in the center of the court. The receiver does have a racquet (see Figure 3-23).

2. *How to perform the drive serve*

a. The purpose of the drive serve is to hit the ball quickly and low, to either the right or left back corner of the court. If hit correctly, it will bounce first just past the short service line and second before it reaches the back wall (Figure 3-23).

b. The server stands in the center of the service area in a forehand stroking position.

c. The ball is dropped near the front service line to allow the server to step to the ball and build momentum.

d. Using a good forehand stroke, the hitter contacts the ball

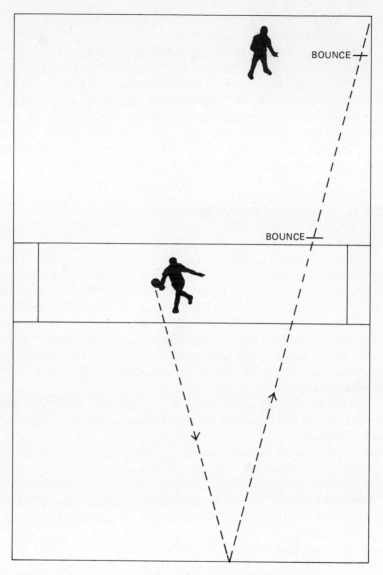

FIGURE 3-23 Drive serve with receiver catching the ball

somewhere in front of the lead foot and between the ankle and the knee in height. This keeps the ball low.

e. The ball should be driven into the front wall at about waist to chest height (the harder the ball is hit, the lower this point on the front wall can be) and approximately one foot left of center. The ball should rebound and hit the floor just past the short service line, traveling toward the left backhand corner of the court.

3. *Receiving the serve*
   a. The receiver watches the server's body position and racquet path and tries to anticipate the direction of the serve.
   b. The receiver moves to a position behind the flight of the ball, and prepares to hit a forehand or backhand stroke.
   c. The receiver attempts to catch the ball with one hand in the position where the racquet would contact the ball.
4. *The task*
   The server attempts five drive serves to the forehand side and five to the backhand side. The receiver catches each serve, and returns it to the server (Figure 3-23).

Task 2: The Half-lob serve
1. *How to perform the half-lob serve*
   a. The purpose of the half-lob serve is to increase the chances of getting a second serve legally into play and also to slow down the pace of the game.
   b. The server stands in the center of the service area, shoulders squarely to the front wall. The foot opposite the racquet hand is slightly forward.
   c. The ball is dropped in front of the body, but is bounced higher than on the drive serve (contact point is chest to head high). The stroke should be a half-swing, with little or no wrist action. It is actually more of a push (Figure 3-24).

FIGURE 3-24 The contact point in the half-lob serve

    d. The ball should contact the front wall at about two feet above head height and one foot to the left of the center of the front wall. It should rebound with a high trajectory and land on the first bounce just past the short service line. The second bounce should carry the ball into the deep left corner.

    e. The half-lob serve, like the drive serve, can be hit to either the left or right rear corner. The angle at which a player hits the front wall and the distance from the center of the front wall are determined by where the player stands in the service area.

2. *Receiving the half-lob serve*

    a. The receiver stands in the same position as when receiving the drive serve and tries to anticipate where the ball will land after the first bounce, moving to a position behind that point.

    b. The receiver attempts to catch the ball with one hand in the position where the racquet would contact the ball.

3. *The task*

The server attempts five half-lob serves to the forehand side and five to the backhand side. The receiver catches each serve and returns it to the server (Figure 3-25).

Task 3: The Drive and Half-lob serves—receiver moves and hits the ball

    The server hits four drive serves, and the receiver tries to return each serve. The server then hits four half-lob serves, and the receiver moves into position to hit a fundamentally correct forehand or backhand stroke.

    CAUTION: Each rally should be composed of only two hits, the serve and one return shot!

D. Evaluation Checklist   YES   NO

1. *Drive Serve*

    a. Assumes a good forehand stroke position

    b. Positions self deep in the service area

    c. Drops ball in front of body to allow for a full swing

    d. Finds the contact point low and in front of lead foot

    e. Drives ball into front wall at a low point to the left of center for a serve to left rear corner

    f. Bounces ball to short service line and angles it directly into the left corner

    g. Swings fundamentally correctly, with good follow-through

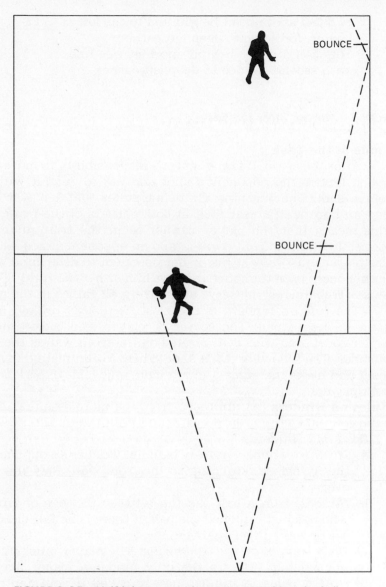

FIGURE 3-25 Half-lob serve with receiver catching the ball

2. *Half-lob Serve*   <u>YES</u>   <u>NO</u>
   a. Stands more upright, facing the front wall
   b. Bounces ball in front of body and high
   c. Finds contact point at chest to head height
   d. Takes a short step and a short swing in
      which ball is pushed to the front wall
   e. Hits ball so that it contacts front wall about

two feet above head height and to the left of <u>YES   NO</u>
center, for serve to deep left corner

  f. Hits ball directly behind short service line,
with second bounce in deep left corner

SESSION 7 Moving after the Serve

A. Value of the Task

      After the serve, it is the server's responsibility to move so as
not to hinder the opponent's shot and not to get hit with the
return shot. The Teaching Guideline states that a player must
give an opponent a clear shot at both corners of the front wall.
This means that the player cannot be in the triangular area
formed by the two front corners and an opponent's racquet face.
The player must *look* at his or her opponent to determine where
the opponent is on the court and give him or her the right-of-way.
This is true during the serve and during all rallies in the game.

      The rule on hinders is the most frequently broken in the
game of racquetball. The server or player who backs into the
center-court area with eyes riveted on the front wall is the main
offender. The following drills should help to eliminate this movement and make the game a much more enjoyable experience for
both players.

B. Rules on Hinders (paraphrased from the more essential AARA
rules)

  1. *Dead Ball Hinders*

    a. *Hitting an opponent.* Any ball that touches an opponent on
the fly before returning to the front wall. Play the point
over.

    b. *Straddle ball.* A ball passing between the legs of a player
who has just returned the ball, if there is no fair chance to
see or return it. Play over.

    c. *Body contact on the backswing.* The player must call this
immediately. This is the only hinder a player may call
(AARA rules: A hinder may be called if you step on an
opponent's foot). Play over.

    d. *Blocking the opponent.* A player is entitled to a fair chance
to see and return the ball. It is the duty of the side that has
just served or returned the ball to move so that the other
side can go straight to the ball without going around an
opponent. Play over (Figure 3-26).

  2. *Avoidable Hinders.* The following instances result in an automatic point or a side-out:

FIGURE 3-26 Following the serve, the server rivets eyes on the front wall, forcing opponent to change his or her shot.

a. *Failure to move.* Does not move sufficiently to allow opponent a shot.
b. *Blocking.* Moving into a position that blocks an opponent who is about to move to the ball.
c. *Moving into the ball.* Player is struck by the ball just played by the opponent.
d. *Pushing.* Deliberately pushing or shoving an opponent during play.

C. Task Practice

Task 1: The Serve—receiver catches the ball

1. One person stands in the center of the service area, the other stands in the center of the backcourt area.
2. The server hits a drive serve to the left back corner. The server must watch the ball to determine where the receiver is hitting it from (Figure 3-27).
3. As a general rule, if the receiver is on the left half of the backcourt, the server must move into the right half of the court to an area as close to the center of the court as possible (Figure 3-28).
4. When the server gets to this position, he or she faces diagonally into the front corner of the half of the court on which the receiver is positioned. The server *looks* at the receiver over one shoulder while the receiver is catching (hitting) the ball. The use of eyeguards makes this a safe and more palatable experience (Figure 3-28).

FIGURE 3-27 Correctly watching the ball during play, thereby avoiding a hinder

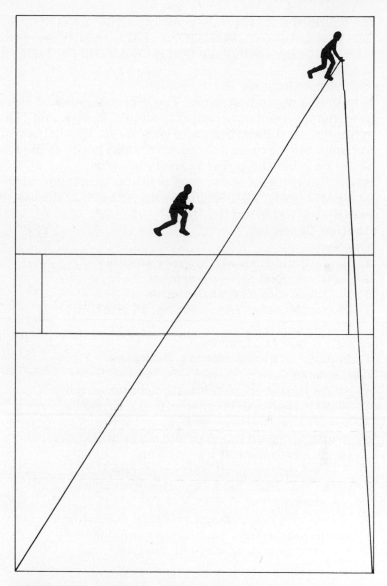

FIGURE 3-28 Moving to correct position on the court and watching opponent following the serve

5. As the receiver begins to swing, the server begins to turn his or her head back toward the front wall, following the flight of the ball. This is where anticipation begins. The server should start to react or get into position for the next shot as soon as he or she *sees* the ball leave the opponent's racquet.

6. The server now hits five drive serves, and the receiver catches

the ball in the appropriate position. STOP AND CHECK THE SERVER'S COURT POSITION. THE RECEIVER SHOULD HAVE A CLEAR SHOT AT BOTH CORNERS OF THE FRONT WALL!

Task 2: Game Situation

1. Now play a regulation game. The server serves and you alternate hits until someone commits a fault. Keep score! The server announces the score prior to each serve. This helps you both to remember the correct score, and it also apprises the receiver of the fact that the server is ready to serve.
2. Be overly critical of your court position, and call hinders freely. REMEMBER, YOU SHOULD BE ABLE TO SEE YOUR OPPONENT CONTACT THE BALL!

D. Evaluation Checklist   YES   NO

1. *The Serve*
   a. Uses a fundamentally correct stroke
   b. Achieves good serve placement
   c. Faults continually on the serve
   d. Moves to the correct position on the court following the serve
   e. Hits a variety of serves
   f. Usually hits to opponent's weakness
2. *The Receiver*
   a. Starts in correct position (the center of the backcourt area about an arm and a racquet's length from the back wall)
   b. Reacts to the direction of the serve quickly, moving into the hitting position
   c. Hits a fundamentally correct stroke
   d. Gets the ball back to the front wall consistently
   e. Moves to a center-court position following the service return that allows opponent a fair shot at both corners of the front wall

SESSION 8   The Forehand Ceiling Ball

A. Value of the Task

The ceiling ball is one of the most important shots in the repertoire of the racquetball player. It is the primary defensive shot, and it can be the first shot in an offensive sequence. The ceiling ball can be used to slow the pace of the game or to allow the hitter time to recover and take over the center-court position.

There are actually two types of ceiling balls. In one, the contact point is between the floor and the shoulders, and it is actually a sidearm swing. The other is an overhand swing in which the contact point is above shoulder height. No matter which shot you choose, the ball should hit the ceiling at a distance of three to four feet from the front wall, then hit the front wall and the floor, and then rebound deep into the backcourt *without* hitting the back wall. Strategically, you should attempt to hit the ball into the deep

FIGURE 3-29 The traditional ready position for the forehand ceiling ball

corner on your opponent's weakest side. WHEN IN DOUBT, GO TO THE CEILING!

B. On-Court Warm-Up
1. Drop-and-Hit Drill (see session 4)
2. Ceiling Ball Footwork Drill (see session 1)

C. Mechanics of the Task (Figures 3-29 and 3-30)
1. *Grip.* Use the regular forehand grip. Some people prefer to use a panhandle grip in which the "V" formed by the thumb and index finger is directly in the middle of the side of the handle.
2. *Stance.* There are actually two options here, although in both instances you should be *behind* the flight of the ball.
    a. Traditional—regular forehand stroking position with shoulders facing the sidewall, left foot forward, and racquet held high. This allows you to transfer your weight from the back to the front foot, giving you more power. This stance is suggested for use with a slower ball.
    b. Squared-off—the shoulders and feet facing the front wall and racquet held high and in front of the shoulder. With this stance the panhandle grip may be more appropriate. The squared-off stance is used with a more lively ball because less force is required and less body is used in this stroke.
3. *Racquet Path.* The arm and the racquet come directly over the shoulder to a straight-arm position at the contact point. At contact, the racquet is at about a forty-five-degree angle, with the face of the racquet turned toward the ceiling (Figure 3-31).
4. *Body Movement.* Take a slight step forward with the foot opposite the racquet arm. There should be a slight weight transfer to the front foot, and the body should be moving forward at contact. Back foot should be planted.
5. *Contact Point.* Contact the ball at a high point, about one foot in *front* of the shoulder. If you contact the ball out to the side or behind the shoulder, you place tremendous stress on the shoulder and elbow. It is much more efficient to hit the ball in front of and in line with the shoulder.
6. *Placement*
    a. Traditional—attempt to hit the ceiling about three or four feet from the front wall. With the slower ball you must stroke through, firmly applying enough force to get the ball to rebound deep in the court.
    b. Squared-off—hit the ceiling about ten to fifteen feet from the front wall, with an easy but firm stroke. The lively ball

FIGURE 3-30 Contact point in front of lead shoulder and about 1 foot in front of the head

FIGURE 3-31   Contact on ceiling ball shot. Angle of racquet face should be forty-five degrees. Note contact in front of dominant shoulder.

will rebound into the deep backcourt with this type of stroke.

D. Task Practice

1. One person stands in each half of the backcourt area. Each person has a ball.
2. Throw the ball high in the air, attempting to hit the ceiling approximately one yard in front of where you are standing. Use an underhand throw. As the ball comes down, move into a position behind the place where it will bounce on the floor. Allow the ball to bounce, and when it gets to a high position, hit a ceiling ball. *Attempt* about ten shots.
3. One player throws the ball underhand, to bounce high off the front wall. The hitter is in the backcourt area. The hitter moves into a position behind the bounce, and hits a ceiling ball to one of the back corners. Reverse positions and repeat, ten each.
4. Both players stand in the backcourt area. Every shot should be a ceiling ball. After hitting, move up to the center-court position while your opponent hits, and then try to continuously rally the ball using ceiling shots.

E. Evaluation Checklist   <u>YES</u>   <u>NO</u>

1. Gets into position behind the flight of the ball
2. Finds contact point in front of, and above, hitting shoulder
3. Contacts with straight arm and racquet at a forty-five-degree angle
4. Directs ball to hit ceiling in appropriate spot
5. Causes ball to end up in deep corner of the court
6. Rotates to center position after hit

SESSION 9   The Backhand Ceiling Ball

A. Value of the Task

The backhand ceiling ball is one of the most difficult shots in the game, and the lack of this skill has been the downfall of many players. Since it is a defensive play, this is the one situation in the game when it is *not* necessarily a mistake to run around your backhand and hit a forehand stroke. However, in every game the occasion will arise when you will be forced to hit a backhand ceiling ball. The more intelligent opponent will strategically place the ball so that you will be forced to hit your weakest shot. Therefore, taking a forehand stroke is not the recommended procedure. Instead, you should work on the development of a good backhand ceiling game to complement your various strengths. There are actually two types of backhand ceiling balls, the waist-high and the overhead. You should be prepared to hit both of these shots when needed.

B. On-Court Warm-Up

1. Ceiling Ball Footwork Drill (see session 1)
2. Drop-and-Hit Drill (using only the backhand stroke)

C. Task Practice

Task 1: Waist-high backhand ceiling ball

1. *Mechanics of the task.* These are the same as those used in the regular backhand stroke, the only difference occurring when you begin to swing. As the racquet begins its forward movement to the contact point, lower your back shoulder to force your swing upward. Just prior to contact, turn your wrist so that the back of the hand points toward the ceiling. Following contact, the racquet follows through to a high finish. Contact the ball in front of your body and at the highest point possible. The same swing can be used for balls that are head high or lower. Just prior to the initiation of the swing, plant your back foot so that it provides you with a stable base for the stroke.

Hit the ball so that it strikes the ceiling at a point three to five feet from the front wall. The ceiling ball is a much more effective shot if it is hit into the deep corners of the court and if it takes its second bounce before it hits the back wall.

2. *The task*
   a. Both players stand in the backcourt area. Drop the ball in front of you, and as it reaches the peak of its bounce, hit a ceiling ball using a backhand stroke. Catch the ball on the rebound, and repeat the task five times.
   b. One person stands in the service area and the other stands in the backcourt area on the backhand side. The player in the front hits the ball about waist high off the front wall to the other player's backhand side. The hitter then executes a backhand ceiling ball. Catch the ball on the rebound, and repeat ten times each.
   c. One person at a time attempts to hit as many continuous backhand ceiling balls as possible.

Task 2: Overhead backhand ceiling ball

1. *Mechanics of the task.* The stance is the same as that used in the regular backhand stroke, emphasizing the turn to the backhand sidewall. The backswing places the racquet and the racquet arm in a position parallel to the shoulders. Initiate the swing by a slight elbow movement forward and upward as you reach for the ball. (Follow the same principles that are used in all swings, going from a bent arm to a straight-arm position.) Simultaneously, begin to move the lead foot forward and plant the back foot. Contact the ball across from your lead shoulder and out to the side. At contact, the racquet face should be flush with the ball and the front wall, angling slightly upward. Hold the wrist action until contact, and then follow through in the direction of the front wall.

   Attempt to hit the ball to a point on the ceiling three to five feet from the front wall. As with the waist-high shot, hit the ball into the deep back corners of the court.

2. *The task*
   a. Both players stand in the deep backcourt area. Using an underhand throw, try to hit the ceiling approximately one yard in front of where you are standing. As the ball comes down, move to a position behind the place where it will bounce on the floor. Allow the ball to bounce, and when it gets to a high position, hit a backhand overhead ceiling ball. Repeat ten times.
   b. One player throws the ball underhand, to bounce high off

the front wall. The hitter, who is in the backcourt area, moves into a position behind the bounce and hits a back-hand overhead ceiling ball to one of the back corners. Reverse positions, and repeat ten times each.

c. One person at a time attempts to hit as many backhand ceiling balls in a row as possible. Use both the waist-high and overhand strokes as needed.

d. With both players in the backcourt area, hit all backhand ceiling balls. After you hit, move up to the center-court position while your opponent hits, and then try to continuously rally the ball using only ceiling shots.

D. Evaluation Checklist   YES   NO

1. *Waist-high backhand ceiling ball*
   a. Stands facing the proper sidewall
   b. Is behind the flight of the ball
   c. Uses effective backhand stroking pattern
   d. Drops back shoulder at contact
   e. Turns wrist up and angles the racquet face (back of hand toward the ceiling)
   f. Shifts weight forward and follows through toward the ceiling
   g. Keeps feet on the floor at contact
   h. Makes sure ball strikes ceiling at three to five feet from front wall
   i. Number of individual continuous ceiling balls _____

2. *Overhead ceiling ball*
   a. Stands facing the correct sidewall
   b. Is behind the flight of the ball
   c. Keeps racquet arm and racquet about parallel to shoulders
   d. Uses elbow to lead the swing forward and up
   e. Contacts ball in line with the lead shoulder and out to the side
   f. Keeps racquet flush with front wall and angled slightly upward
   g. Exhibits good follow-through upward
   h. Makes sure ball hits ceiling three to five feet from front wall
   i. Keeps feet in contact with floor during the stroke
   j. Continuous backhand overhead ceiling balls _____

SESSION 10   Passing Shots

A. Value of the Task

The passing shot is an excellent supplement to most individuals' games and is essential for the person who has difficulty killing the ball. It can be used to score an outright winner or to force your opponent to chase the ball into the backcourt area and possibly hit a weak return. Passing shots are usually hit when your opponent is in front of you, is parallel to you, or is caught on one side of the court. When any of these situations arises, you have the option of using any one of three different passing shots. The *cross-court pass,* or "V" pass, sends the ball out of reach of your opponent and directly into the opposite deep back corner of the court. The *down-the-wall pass* takes the ball down and back, parallel to one of the sidewalls. The *wide-angle pass* is supposed to hit the sidewall at a point parallel to your opponent's position and rebound into the backcourt area. In all three of these shots, the ball should be hit to a point about two feet up on the front wall in order to eliminate the possibility of the balls reaching the back wall, from where it may easily be returned.

B. On-Court Warm-Up

Drop and hit to spots. One person hits forehands and the other backhands. Tape shapes on the front wall or use existing lines as targets for practicing accuracy. You may also use ball cans or racquet covers on the floor to indicate the target. Attempt to hit various targets with your shots, keeping the ball about two feet off the floor, to simulate the passing shot. Hit ten shots each, then switch sides and repeat.

C. Mechanics of the Task (cross-court and wide-angle passes)

The wide-angle pass is simply a variation of the cross-court pass, and therefore the mechanics are exactly the same. The only differences lie in the angle of flight and in the placement of the two shots.

1. *Basic Stroke.* This should be exactly the same as your regular forehand and backhand strokes. If you are having some difficulty getting the ball to cross the court, you may want to open up your stance at contact to help you pull the ball over to the opposite side.

2. *Contact Point.* To hit a cross-court or wide-angle pass, you have to hit the ball a little more forward in your stance. This allows the racquet head to start to turn in the given direction before you actually contact the ball. Since this is not a kill shot, it is possible to contact the ball at a higher point in its flight. The ball can be contacted somewhere between knee and

waist height and still made to hit the front wall at a height of two to three feet.

3. *The Angle.* Your position on the court dictates where you must hit the front wall in order to execute a good passing shot. In general, if you are going to hit a cross-court pass, you must

FIGURE 3-32 The cross-court pass

hit the ball to the front wall at a point which is half the distance from the sidewall and the place on the front wall that is directly across from your racquet. To hit a wide-angle pass from the same position, you must hit the ball past this halfway point, so that the ball hits the sidewall as it passes your opponent (Figures 3-32 and 3-33).

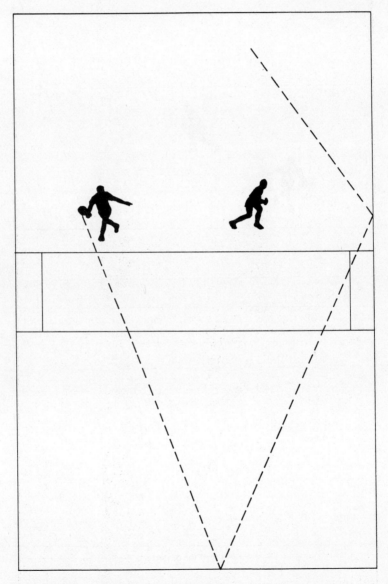

FIGURE 3-33   The wide-angle pass

D. Task Practice

1. Use the same basic court organization for practicing both passing shots. One person stands in the center court position and the other person stands either on the backhand or forehand side and slightly behind the first person.
2. The person in the center-court area hits the ball easily off the front wall at about waist height to set up the person hitting the pass. The person hitting the passing shot must determine the correct angle and then hit either a cross-court or wide-angle pass. The person in center court watches the point at which the ball hits the front wall, in order to adjust this point to correct the shot. Hit ten forehands and ten backhands and then switch.

E. Common Errors

1. The ball does not pass your opponent but hits the sidewall and rebounds into center court for an easy setup. *Correction:* If this occurs on a cross-court pass, you must *decrease* the angle at which the ball hits the front wall. If it occurs on a wide-angle pass, you must also *decrease* the angle but not as much as in correcting the cross-court pass.
2. The ball passes your opponent but carries all the way to the back wall, where it can be retrieved or shot. *Correction:* You must hit the ball to a lower point on the front wall. The guideline is approximately two to three feet high, but this depends on how hard you hit the ball. The harder you hit, the lower the point on the front wall. Also check your contact point. If you are hitting the ball waist high or above, this could result in a high passing shot. Let the ball drop, and contact it at a lower point in its flight.

SESSION 11 The Pinch Shot

A. Value of the Task

The pinch shot is used to take advantage of an opponent who remains in the deep-court area, who is out of position, or who continually places his or her body weight on the heels (he or she is planted in a position on the court). The pinch shot hits the sidewall and then the front wall, or the front wall and then the sidewall, thereby slowing the ball down, changing its direction, and keeping it in the extreme front-court area. It is a very effective shot to use in rallies in which the ball is continually hit straight up and down the court. The pinch shot is an excellent complement to your passing game, and, when used in combination with your other shots, it can keep your opponent off-balance both physically and mentally.

B. On-Court Warm-Up

1. *Drop-and-Hit Drill.* One person stands on each side of the court behind the short service line. Drop the ball from about waist height, and attempt to hit it *before* it hits the floor. Hit ten forehands and ten backhands.

2. Throw the ball to the back wall and hit it after it has bounced once. Hit five forehands and five backhands.

C. Mechanics of the Task

1. *Grip.* Use your regular forehand or backhand grip. With the pinch shot, it is critical that you have a firm grip at the contact point.

2. *Stance.* Use your normal forehand or backhand stance.

3. *Backswing.* This is the same as the regular forehand or backhand backswing.

4. *Position on the Court.* Most experts say that the shot is usually more effective if you are in the front-court area and your opponent is in the backcourt area. My opinion is that the shot can be hit effectively from any position on the court and should depend upon your opponent's location, movement skills, and where his or her weight is being borne. If your opponent does not watch the ball when it is behind him or her, or if your opponent is between you and a sidewall, and you hit the ball directly to the sidewall near which he or she is standing, the pinch shot is effective. If you are parallel to your opponent from the short service line back, the pinch shot can be an effective alternative.

5. *Path of the Racquet.* This is the same as your regular forehand and backhand stroke.

6. *Contact Point. This is the element that differentiates the pinch shot from most other strokes.* You should contact the ball a little deeper in your stance, from about the midline of your body back. This will force you to hit the ball with an open racquet face, sending the ball into the sidewall. You can hit the sidewall at varying distances from the front wall, depending upon the situation and your opponent's position. Usually the most effective pinch shot hits the sidewall anywhere from one yard to one inch from the front wall (Figure 3-34).

7. *Wrist Action.* In order to keep the racquet face open at the contact point, you should delay your wrist action. After contact, you can explode with the wrist in a normal fashion.

8. *Follow-through.* This is the same as in a regular forehand or backhand stroke.

FIGURE 3-34 The contact point for the pinch shot. Deeper in the stance, it forces you to hit the ball with an open racquet face.

D. Task Practice

1. One person hits, the other retrieves. Stand in the center-court area, and drop-hit pinch shots. Hit ten forehands and then ten backhands. Remember to drop the ball so that it is in the middle of your stance after you have taken your forward step. Hit the ball as if you were going to stroke a normal forehand or backhand kill shot. Repeat with your partner hitting.

2. Your opponent stands approximately six feet behind you, between you and a sidewall. He or she throws or easily hits the ball parallel to the sidewall near which he or she is standing. You should return the ball by hitting a pinch shot directly into the sidewall closest to your opponent (Figures 3-35 and 3-36).

3. Play a modified game in which you hit pinch shots whenever the occasion presents itself.

4. If you are alone on the court, practice forehand and backhand pinches by standing behind the short service line and continually rallying and alternating from the forehand to the backhand side.

E. Common Errors

1. Ball hits the sidewall but skips before it gets to the front wall. *Correction:* You must stroke the ball *firmly.* You cannot let up

on the stroke and push, poke, or guide the ball to the front wall. It must be a complete stroke. You may also have to hit the ball higher on the sidewall and closer to the front wall.

2. Difficulty hitting the sidewall first. *Correction:* You are probably hitting the ball too far forward in your stance. Let the ball

FIGURE 3-35 Pinch shot hitting the wall that opponent is standing near

get into the middle of your stance before you hit it. Try to delay your wrist action so that the racquet face remains open prior to reaching the contact point. Remember this is a kill shot, so you must have a low contact point and hit the ball to a low position on the sidewall.

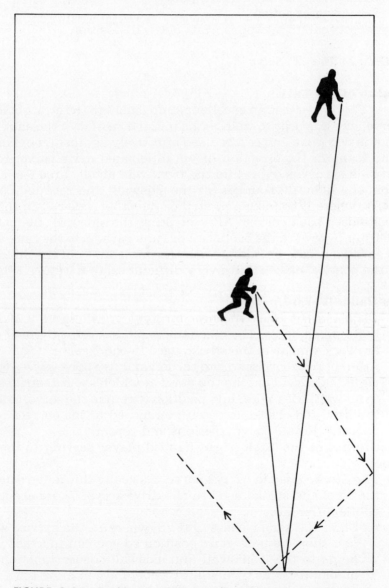

FIGURE 3-36 Backhand pinch taking advantage of opponent's court position

F. Evaluation Checklist　　　　　　　　　　　　　　　YES　　NO
1. Assumes a good forehand or backhand stance
2. Uses a complete stroke, not a push or poke
3. Makes sure the contact point is behind the center of the body
4. Grips firmly at the contact point
5. Delays wrist action
6. Directs ball to hit appropriate sidewall position

SESSION 12　The "Z" Serve

A. Value of the Task

The "Z" serve is an excellent supplement to the straight drive serve, and it is used to change the initial direction of the shot. The shot is deceptive and can be used effectively against an opponent who leans in the direction of an anticipated drive serve. If the serve is hit correctly, it hits the front wall about three feet away from the sidewall, bounces off the sidewall, and rebounds cross court, where it bounces and strikes the other sidewall in the opposite deep back corner. After striking the sidewall, the ball either jumps toward the back wall or runs parallel to the back wall. The initial deception, along with the uncertainty of the direction of the bounce, makes this a very difficult serve to return (Figure 3-37).

B. On-Court Warm-Up
1. *Drop-and-Hit Drill.* Attempt straight-in kill shots and forehand pinch shots. The mechanics of the forehand pinch shot are very similar to the stroke used in the Z serve.
2. Attempt five drive serves to the left and five drive serves to the right. Opponent checks the point at which the ball strikes the front wall, tries to get into position to return the serve, catches the ball, and checks to see if you moved to the correct court position. Rotate court positions and repeat.

C. Mechanics of the Task (right-handed player serving to the left side)
1. *The Stroke Used to Hit a Z Serve.* Basically this is the same as the forehand stroke used in the drive serve. There are a few subtle differences:
   a. Since the server can stand anywhere in the service zone, you should adjust your position so you can increase your angle to the front wall and sidewall corner junction. To accomplish this, you will probably have to move to the left of the center of the zone. Try to stand in a position that allows you to hit several different types of serves, so that

your opponent will not be forewarned that a Z serve is coming.

b. The ball must be dropped so that *after* you have taken your step toward the front corner, the ball is approximately in the middle of your stance. This helps you to hit the ball with an open racquet face and therefore increases your

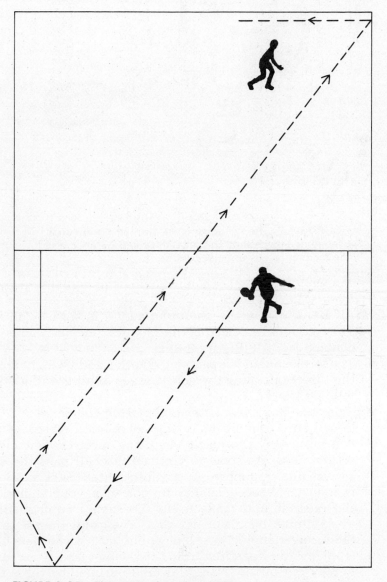

FIGURE 3-37 The path of the "Z" serve

FIGURE 3-38 The "Z" serve is hit with the same stroke used for the pinch shot. The ball is deep in the stance, and the racquet face is open at contact.

chances of hitting the ball into the front right corner of the front wall.

   c. At the contact point, the wrist action is slightly delayed. This too aids in keeping the racquet face open when you contact the ball (Figure 3-38).

   d. The stroke should be completed with a solid weight shift in the direction toward which you are aiming and a strong follow-through.

  2. *Appropriate Movement After Completing the Serve*

   a. Your court position following completion of the serve is determined by the place where the receiver contacts the return shot. As soon as you see the ball pass the short service line, you move quickly into center-court position. It is then your responsibility to look over your shoulder at the receiver and make minor positional adjustments to avoid hindering his or her shot. The guidelines state that the receiver should have a clear shot at both corners of the front wall as measured from the racquet face. Your task is to stay out of the triangular area outlined by these three points. If the ball does end up in the deep left corner, the server should be on the right side of the center of the court behind the short service line (Figure 3-39).

D. Task Practice

1. *Serve—move—catch.* The server hits a Z serve to the opponent's backhand side. The server then moves to the appropri-

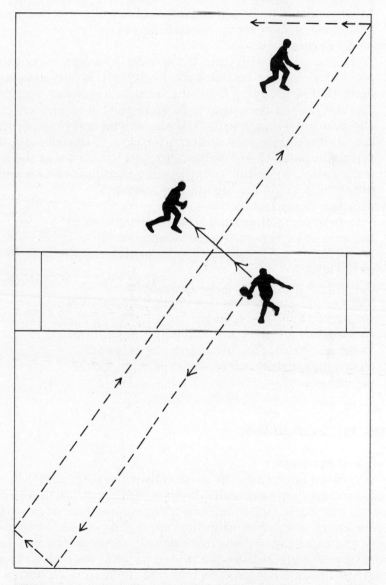

FIGURE 3-39 Movement of the server after the "Z" serve. Notice that the server is not blocking the opponent's shot.

ate position on the court as the receiver catches the ball. The server should *see* the receiver catch the ball! Hit ten serves and then rotate.

2. *Serve—move—return serve.* Go through the same procedure as in point 1 and return the serve. Hit ten serves and returns, rotate, and repeat.

3. Attempt to mix drive serves and Z serves. The receiver returns all serves. Hit ten serves, rotate, and repeat.

E. Common Errors

1. The serve continually hits three walls. *Correction:* Lower the point at which the ball hits the front wall. It may also help to move that point away from the front and sidewall junction.

2. The ball doesn't land deep enough in the backcourt area, usually resulting in a setup. *Correction:* The ball may be hitting the front wall at a point which is too close to the sidewall. Move this point on the front wall out toward the center of the court. It may also be possible to move your serving position and improve your angle for hitting the Z serve.

F. Evaluation Checklist   YES   NO

1. Stands in correct position in the service area to increase the angle to the front-wall corner

2. Drops ball in the range of the middle to the back of the stance

3. Contacts ball with an open racquet face

4. Makes sure ball passes the short line between the server and the receiver

5. Causes the ball to bounce and travel to the deep backcourt area prior to hitting the sidewall

6. Moves into correct center-court position following the serve

SESSION 13   The Splat Shot

A. Value of the Task

Your opponent has hit an excellent passing shot that is extremely close to the sidewall. You move into position to return the shot in the deep backcourt area. Your opponent relaxes in the center-court area, awaiting the impending weak return. You drive the ball directly into the sidewall about one or two feet in front of you, and it rebounds toward the front wall with a tremendous amount of sidespin. The ball hits the front wall with a loud "splat" and rebounds in a line almost parallel to the front wall. It remains in the front court and results in a rally ender. Your opponent is left standing with a confused look on his or her face.

The splat shot is an excellent answer to those difficult-to-return balls that are three inches to three feet away from the sidewall. It differs from the pinch shot in that it is contacted closer to the sidewall and it generates a tremendous amount of spin, causing the ball to rebound at a very sharp angle. The ability to execute the splat allows you to hit an offensive rather than a defensive return. To achieve the desired effect, you must have a sound fundamental forehand or backhand shot. The ball must be driven strongly and firmly into the sidewall, or it will never reach the front wall. The splat is a spectacular shot that can add points to your game and help to move you up through the levels of play.

B. On-Court Warm-Up
1. *Straight-in, Drop-and-Hit Drill* (see session 4). You hit forehands and the other person hits backhands. Hit ten shots each, and then switch sides.
2. *Drop-and-Hit Pinch Shots.* You hit forehands and the other person hits backhands. Hit ten shots each, and then switch.

C. Mechanics of the Task
1. *Grip.* Use your regular forehand or backhand grip. It is critical to have a firm grip at the contact point.
2. *Stance.* Use your normal forehand or backhand stance.
3. *Backswing.* This is the same as in the regular forehand or backhand stroke.
4. *Racquet Movement.* This follows as in your regular stroke.
5. *Contact Point.* It should be low and fall from slightly in front to slightly in back of the midpoint of your swing (Figure 3-40).
6. *Wrist Action.* It is important that the wrist action remain the same as it is with the regular stroke. It is critical that your wrist be firm at contact and that you *drive* through the ball as you direct it toward the sidewall.
7. *Follow-through.* Similar to that used in your regular forehand or backhand stroke, this should be very strong.
8. *Position on the Court.* This is the major difference between the splat and the pinch shot. The splat is hit from the backcourt area and within three feet of the sidewall. The ball is hit into the sidewall at a distance of from one to five feet in front of the person performing the shot (Figure 3-41). The closer the ball is to the sidewall, the more quickly it should hit the sidewall on its way to the front wall. Therefore if you are standing three feet away from the sidewall when you hit the ball, it

FIGURE 3-40 Hitting the splat shot. The ball should be contacted deep in the stance, allowing the player to drive the ball into the sidewall.

should strike the sidewall about five feet in front of you. If you are within three to four inches of the wall at contact, the ball should travel almost directly into the sidewall from the contact point.

D. Task Practice

Task 1

1. The hitter stands on the forehand side in the backcourt area, approximately three feet away from the sidewall. The opponent stands near the short service line on the backhand side of the court (Figure 3-41).
2. The hitter drops the ball and hits ten forehand splat shots. Vary the hitting distance from the sidewall to from three inches to three feet.
3. The opponent retrieves all attempts and returns the ball to the hitter. Reverse positions and repeat.

Task 2

Use the same basic setup as in drill 1, with the hitter performing a backhand splat. Repeat ten times, and reverse roles.

Task 3

Play a controlled game, using the splat shot when it is appropriate.

E. Evaluation Checklist   <u>YES</u>   NO

   1. Assumes correct stance

   2. Makes sure the ball is close enough to the sidewall to make the splat shot a valid option

   3. Finds the contact point somewhere from

FIGURE 3-41 The splat shot is driven into the sidewall, and the spin that is generated causes it to squirt across the front court.

slightly in front to slightly behind the middle   <u>YES</u>   <u>NO</u>
of the swing
4. Uses a firm grip and stroke
5. Hits the ball off the sidewall with force and at
   an appropriate distance from the hitter
6. Maintains a strong follow-through

SESSION 14   The Overhead Shots (Drive, Kill, Pinch)

A. Value of the Task

The ability to execute a variety of overhead shots takes on
more meaning as the player begins to adopt an aggressive offensive style of play. The stroking pattern for all overhead options is
very similar to that used in the tennis serve or in the badminton
smash, that is, the ball is driven down toward the junction of the
floor and the front wall. The overhead can be used to break up
seemingly endless ceiling rallies or to pick up the pace of the
game. The shot is usually hit from the backcourt area and is
either driven down the wall past an opponent, killed, or, in a case
where both players are in the backcourt section, pinched. Overheads are advanced shots and should not be added to your arsenal
until you have developed accuracy and consistency with the more
fundamental shots.

B. On-Court Warm-Up

1. Ceiling Ball Footwork Drill (see session 1)
2. Forehand overhead ceiling balls (see session 8, Task Practice
   d.)

C. Mechanics of the Task (Figure 3-42)

1. *Grip and Stance.* These are the same as for the forehand overhead ceiling ball (Figures 3-29 and 3-30).
2. *Racquet Path.* The arm and the racquet come directly over the
   shoulder. The arm is bent until it reaches a straight-arm position at the contact point.
3. *Contact Point.* The ball should be contacted in *front* of the
   shoulder and about one foot lower than for the ceiling ball
   shot. The racquet face should be over the top of the ball and
   angled down toward the floor (Figure 3-43).
4. *Weight Transfer.* Body weight shifts from the back to the
   front foot as you step and rotate your hips during the swing.
5. *Follow-through.* After striking the ball, the racquet should
   continue toward the floor as the wrist and forearm rotate toward the body. This internal rotation keeps the racquet face

FIGURE 3-42 The straight overhead drive, kill, and pinch shots.
The racquet comes directly over
the dominant shoulder and contacts the ball with the face flat.

FIGURE 3-43 Contact point for overhead shots.
The racquet face must be angled down at contact to
produce overhead kill shots and winning passes.
Note that the ball is contacted at a lower point than
in the ceiling ball and well in front of the body.

traveling in the direction of the shot, adds power, and eliminates a slicing effect.

6. *Placement.* The placement of the overhead shot is determined by the same guidelines governing the use of any shot. The place where the shot should hit the front wall is determined by your position on the court and the anticipated direction of the shot. Down-the-wall passes should be hit parallel to the side-walls. Cross-court kills or passes should hit the front wall at a point which is half the distance between your racquet at contact and the sidewall toward which you are hitting (Figure 3-32).

The *overhead kill shot* is hit in exactly the same fashion as the overhead drive, except that you allow the ball to drop a little lower in its flight before hitting it. This directs the ball to a position closer to the juncture of the front wall and the floor. This is obviously a very difficult shot and shouldn't be used very frequently by a player at any level. Traditional theory calls for racquetball shots to be contacted at a low point in order to increase the percentage of roll-outs. Your margin of error in executing kill shots decreases as the height of the contact point increases. Contacting the ball at its highest point and hitting an unusually high number of overhead shots is indicative of beginning and lower-level players.

D. Task Practice

Drill 1. The person performing the overhead shot stands in the backcourt area on the forehand side, about an arm and a racquet's length away from the sidewall. The partner stands parallel to the hitter, near the center of the court, and throws or lightly hits the ball about three-quarters of the way up the front wall. As the ball rebounds, the hitter moves to a position behind the anticipated contact point and hits a down-the-wall overhead passing shot, attempting to hit the ball parallel to the sidewall and at a height of one or two feet. Repeat ten times, and then reverse positions (Figure 3-44).

Drill 2. Move to the backhand side of the court. The hitter is one arm's length from the sidewall on the backhand side, facing the front-wall, forehand corner of the court as though about to hit a forehand stroke. The thrower stands near the center-court area and parallel to the hitter. The thrower lightly hits or throws the ball three-quarters of the way up the front wall and, on the rebound, the hitter moves into position behind the ball and hits an overhead passing shot down the backhand wall. Repeat ten times, and reverse positions (Figure 3-45).

Drill 3. Using the same setup as for drills 1 and 2, the hitter attempts to hit cross-court overhead passing shots. Review the description of the skill, and then perform ten shots from the forehand side and ten from the backhand side of the court.

Drill 4. Begin a ceiling ball rally. After each ceiling ball, the hitter should return to center-court position. When the ceiling ball comes up short in the court, try to hit a down-the-wall over-

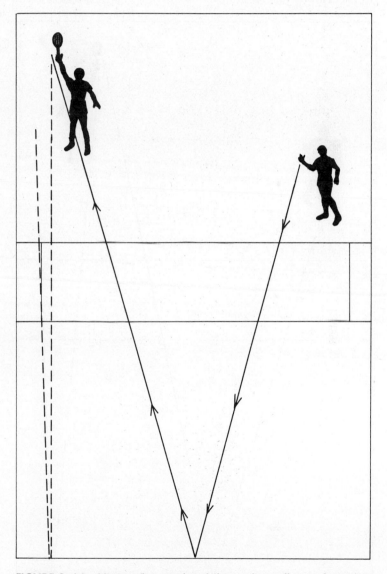

FIGURE 3-44   Hitting the overhead down-the-wall pass from the forehand side of the court

head shot. If your opponent can retrieve the shot, hit a ceiling ball. Repeat for five to ten minutes.

E. Evaluation Checklist   <u>YES</u>   <u>NO</u>

1. Uses correct forehand ceiling ball stance
2. Makes sure ball comes down in *front* of him or her

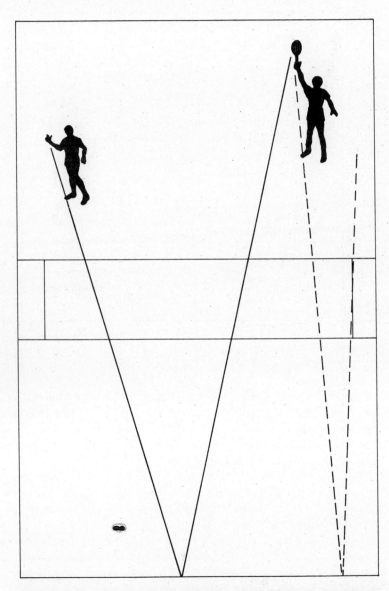

FIGURE 3-45   The overhead pass shot drill from the backhand side of the court

3. Angles the racquet face down at contact (If the   YES   NO
   ball is going up or is too high on the front wall,
   the racquet face is probably up at contact. Correct this by allowing the ball to drop further
   prior to contact.)
4. Follows through down and away from the
   body, not across the body
5. Causes the ball to strike the front wall at a
   height of two feet or less from the floor

SESSION 15   The Overhead Round-the-Head Shot

A. Value of the Task

The overhead shots covered to this point have all been hit
from the forehand side. If you follow the same principles, you can
hit the same shots from the backhand side. However, for most
people the backhand stroke is extremely difficult. Overhead
strokes are low-percentage shots. Add to this the difficulty encountered on the backhand side, and the percentages rapidly decrease. When the ball has to be returned from the extreme backhand side (one foot away from the wall), you may be able to
increase your success by hitting a variation of the forehand
stroke called a round-the-head shot. All overhead shots are possible with this stroke, but it is especially efficient when hitting
opposite-corner pinches. This is due to the fact that, with the
round-the-head shot, the angle of the racquet face at contact is
toward the opposite front corner. If you can execute this shot, it
adds another dimension to your game, another option that your
opponent must anticipate on ceiling ball returns.

B. On-Court Warm-Up

1. Overhead ceiling balls (see session 8, Task Practice 4)
2. Overhead cross-court passes (see session 14, Task Practice 3)

C. Mechanics of the Task

1. *Grip and Stance.* These are the same as for the forehand overhead ceiling ball (Figures 3-29 and 3-30).
2. *Position of the Body in Relation to the Ball.* The right-handed
   player lines up as if for a forehand overhead shot. The critical
   difference is that the ball should come down in *front* of the *left*
   shoulder (Figure 3-46).
3. *Body Movement.* Body weight begins to shift from the back
   foot to the front foot during the swing. It is beneficial to arch
   the back and bend slightly to the left side (if right-handed)
   during the initiation of the stroke.
4. *Racquet Path.* The racquet travels from the cocked ready posi-

FIGURE 3-46   Contact point for the round-
the-head shot. This is in front of and to the
outside of the nondominant shoulder.

tion up over the left shoulder to contact the ball. Just prior to
contact, the wrist and the racquet begin to rotate toward the
body and follow through diagonally down across the front of
the body to the right side.

5. *Contact Point.* This should be slightly higher than the head
   and six to twelve inches in front of the left shoulder (Figure
   3-47).
6. *Placement.* The ball travels downward and should hit the sidewall approximately 1½ feet away from the front wall and

FIGURE 3-47 Contact point for
the around-the-head shot

about 1 foot off the floor. The ball continues to the front wall
and moves across the court to the backhand side (Figure 3-48).

D. Task Practice
Task 1
    The hitter stands in the backcourt area on the backhand
side. The other player stands parallel to the hitter and in the
center-court area. The other player throws or lightly hits the ball
about three-quarters of the way up the front wall and to the backhand side of the hitter. The ball rebounds about three-quarters of
the way into the court. The hitter moves into position behind the
anticipated contact point in a forehand stance and hits a round-
the-head pinch shot to the opposite front corner. Repeat ten
times, and reverse roles. The other player should evaluate stroke
mechanics during the drill.
Task 2
    The players are in the same relative positions as in the pre-
vious task. The hitter now mixes overhead ceiling balls, drive
shots, and round-the-head pinch shots. The other player works
on anticipating, retrieving, and returning the shots to the ceiling
on the backhand side. Continue to hit until you feel comfortable
with these options, and then reverse roles and repeat.
Task 3
    Play a regulation game and utilize the round-the-head pinch
shot as the occasion arises.

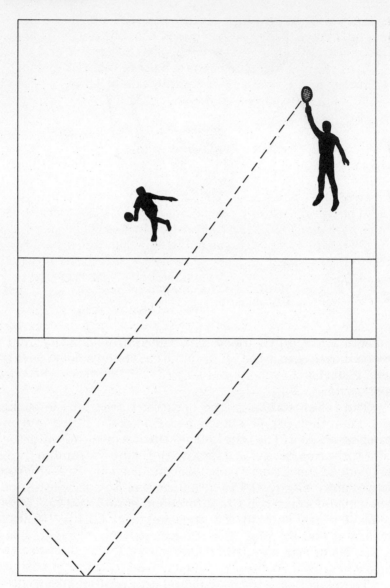

FIGURE 3-48 The angle of the around-the-head pinch shot hit from the backhand side of the court

E. **Evaluation Checklist**   YES   NO
1. Assumes a forehand stance (left foot in front for the right-handed player)
2. Gets *behind* the ball at contact
3. Contacts the ball over and in front of the *left* shoulder

4. Follows through to the right-hand side   YES   NO
5. Sends the ball down and across court (If the ball is not traveling downward, check to determine if the racquet face is over the top of the ball and angled downward at the contact point. Allow the ball to drop lower prior to contact.)

SESSION 16 The Overhead Pinch Shots (Overhead Slice)

A. Value of the Task

The basic strategy in racquetball is to control the center-court position. One of the best methods of moving your opponent out of center court is to hit a ceiling ball. Therefore, in every game there will be several ceiling ball rallies. As the game wears on and the players' fitness level wears down, they get lazy during these rallies, and, instead of returning to center court after hitting a ceiling ball, they remain in the backcourt area. When you feel that your opponent is anticipating your continually hitting ceiling balls, a deceptive overhead pinch will catch him or her standing still and will result in an outright winner. This shot, when used correctly, forces your opponent to cover the entire court and complements your other shots.

B. On-Court Warm-Up

1. Ceiling Ball Footwork Drill (see session 1)
2. Forehand overhead ceiling balls (see session 8, Task Practice 4)
3. Overhead Drive Shot Drill (see session 14, Practice Drill 3)

C. Mechanics of the Task

1. *Grip and Stance.* This is the same as that used for the overhead ceiling ball and the overhead drive or kill shot (Figures 3-29 and 3-30).
2. *Racquet Path.* The backswing brings the racquet to a cocked position behind the shoulder, similar to the arm position before making an overhand throw. The racquet is then brought up toward the ball, and, just prior to contact, the wrist action begins. The wrist action is the same as that involved in turning a doorknob. The follow-through carries the racquet down and across the body.
3. *Contact Point.* The ball is approximately one foot in front of the dominant shoulder and at combined arm and racquet's reach. The racquet slices across the ball at this point, giving it a counterclockwise spin and directing it toward the opposite front corner (Figure 3-49).

FIGURE 3-49 Contact point for the overhead slice pinch. Note the angle of the racquet face at contact as it slices across the ball.

4. *Weight Transfer.* Body weight shifts from the back to the front foot as the swing is performed.
5. *Placement.* The opponent attempts to hit the ceiling ball into one of the back corners of the court. If the ball is in the right corner, the right-handed player then hits the overhead slice pinch cross-court to the left front corner. The ball is on its downward flight as it strikes the sidewall. The ball hits the side wall about one foot up from the floor and at a distance of one or two feet from the front wall, rebounds to the front wall, and remains in the front-court area (Figure 3-50).

D. Task Practice

Task 1

The person who is going to hit the ball should stand in the backcourt area on the forehand side. The other person stands parallel to the hitter, near the center of the court, and throws or lightly hits the ball about three-quarters of the way up the front wall. The ball should bounce and rebound to a position about three-quarters of the way back into the court. The hitter moves into a position behind the anticipated contact point and hits a cross-court overhead slice pinch shot. Repeat ten times, and switch roles. Players should evaluate stroke mechanics during drill.

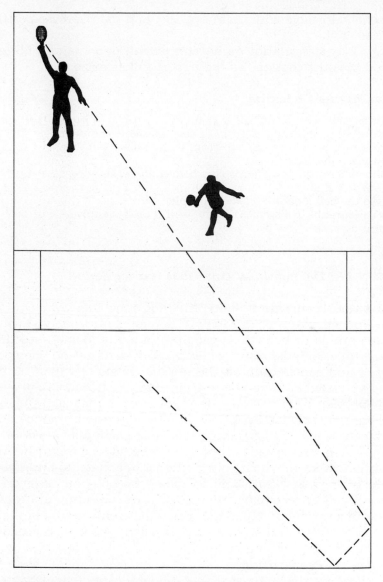

FIGURE 3-50   The overhead slice pinch from the forehand side of the court

Task 2

Set up in the same manner as in the previous drill. The hitter now attempts to mix ceiling balls, overhead drives, and overhead slice pinch shots. The other player works on hitting ceiling ball returns to the deep forehand corner. Continue to hit until both

feel comfortable with these options, and then reverse positions.
Task 3

Play a regulation game, concentrating on using ceiling balls and the other options as the opportunities arise.

E. Evaluation Checklist   YES   NO

1. Stands well behind the ball at contact
2. Contacts the ball high in *front* of the dominant shoulder
3. Slices racquet across the ball from right side to left side just prior to contact
4. Follows through down across the body and carries across to the left side
5. Gives the ball a counterclockwise spin
6. Makes sure the ball strikes the sidewall at the appropriate point

SESSION 17   The Individual One-Hour Practice Period

As you become more competitive and show improvement in your game, you will reach a stage in your development when you will want to accelerate your growth in racquetball skills. Sometimes the best method of accomplishing a growth spurt is to get on the court by yourself and concentrate on the strokes or shots which have been giving you trouble. If you have decided to practice alone, it is a good idea to preplan your session so that you can get the maximum benefit from the time spent. The following is a suggested practice session, which can be modified to emphasize your particular areas of weakness. Almost every aspect of the game should be covered in order to strengthen areas in which your skills are adequate, to improve areas in which they are weak, and to make the one-hour session more interesting. As you explore the use of your forehand and backhand strokes in a variety of situations, you will become more familiar with their possibilities and will be able to adapt them to the changing positions of the bouncing ball.

A. Precourt Preparation
1. Perform the suggested warm-up exercises from Chapter 6.
2. Preplan your session. Cover five or six different skills during the hour. Devote five to ten minutes to each skill.
3. Review the sessions covering the skills you are going to work on. *Pay particular attention* to the sections on mechanics of the skills. Attempt to visualize their correct performance. It may be beneficial to be prepared to analyze each skill in terms of its
   a. Grip
   b. Stance

    c. Backswing
    d. Racquet path
    e. Eye focus
    f. Contact point
    g. Body movement
    h. Wrist snap
    i. Follow-through
    j. Placement

Use the ball as your *cue* to whether or not you are performing the skill correctly. If it is going where it is supposed to, you are probably doing the correct thing. If not, you must discover which aspect of the swing is causing the problem, and then work on correcting it.

REMEMBER, CONCENTRATION IS THE KEY TO IMPROVEMENT!

B. The One-Hour Practice Session

  1. *Drop-and-Hit Drill* (10 minutes)

    a. *Forehand.* Starting behind the short service line, drop and hit the ball using a good forehand stroke, catch the rebound, and repeat. As you feel more comfortable, progressively move back until you are hitting in the range of thirty-five to forty feet. Spend about half of the time hitting the ball after it has bounced and the other half hitting it before it hits the floor. Start hitting the ball with an easy stroke, and increase the velocity as you feel comfortable. Try to hit the ball so that it contacts the front wall within at least one foot of the floor (5 minutes).

    b. *Backhand.* Repeat the drills used for the forehand (5 minutes).

  2. *Back-wall shots* (10 minutes)

    a. *Forehand.* Stand in the center of the backcourt area. Hit the ball high on the front wall so that it bounces once and rebounds off the back wall. Set up and hit a forehand stroke directly to the front wall (5 minutes).

    b. *Backhand.* Repeat the same drills as for the forehand (5 minutes).

  3. *Ceiling balls and kill shots* (10 minutes)

    a. *Forehand.* Start in the deep backcourt area. Hit a waist-high ceiling ball, and as it comes back, return it with an overhead or a waist-high forehand ceiling ball. If the ceiling ball is a poor one (off the back wall or short), try a kill shot (5 minutes).

    b. *Backhand.* Repeat the same drills as for the forehand (5 minutes).

  4. *Serves* (5 to 10 minutes)

    a. Try to hit the four types of serves from the same position in the service zone. Concentrate on where you are standing, where the ball is hitting the front wall, and the end result. Move to various positions in the service zone and practice the four serves.

5. *Sidewall, front-wall pinch shots* (10 minutes)
   a. Stand in the center-court area and drop-hit ten forehand and ten backhand pinch shots.
   b. Stand in the same position and hit the ball off the front wall. As it rebounds, hit a pinch shot. Hit ten forehand and ten backhand shots.
   c. From the same position, try to continuously rally the ball by alternating forehand and backhand pinch shots.

6. *Setups and kill shots* (5 to 10 minutes)
   a. Stand about three-fourths of the way back in the court. Hit the ball so that it rebounds off the front wall and into the backcourt area. Move away from the ball so that it drops to a low position, allowing for a low contact point. Try to hit ten forehand and ten backhand kill shots.
   b. From the same position, hit the ball so that it contacts the front wall and then the sidewall, bounces, and rebounds into the backcourt area. Move away from the ball and set up and hit a kill shot. Attempt ten forehand and ten backhand shots.

C. Postpractice Session

1. Repeat the stretching exercises.
2. Think about your practice session. If any of the shots gave you particular problems, go back and review the appropriate session(s) trying to determine where the problem occurred and what caused it.
3. Watch advanced players perform the skills that gave you problems, analyze their performance, and compare it to your own. This should help you determine your areas of weakness.
4. Incorporate your newly honed skills into the next match that you play.

SESSION 18 Evaluation During Play

The practice sessions have all been designed to develop fundamental skills in a structured drill-type setting and to help you use these skills in controlled situational rallies. Unfortunately you will find that the game is not as structured as this; rather it is composed of a series of seemingly uncontrolled bouts of activity. Therefore it is not uncommon to find individuals who possess beautiful strokes and court movement in these structured sessions but who cannot function effectively in a regulation game. This phenomenon makes it essential that a considerable amount of time be devoted to actual play and evaluation of player's responses in this open or unstructured setting.

The following evaluation sheet can be used to evaluate your play or as a guide for the observation of the game plan of advanced players. (It is strongly recommended that you do several guided observations of players on both your own and more advanced levels of play so that you can contrast game skills and strategies.) The evaluation sheet can then become the starting point for a program to further improve your overall game.

RACQUETBALL: GAME ANALYSIS

PLAYER 1 _____ PLAYER 2 _____ DATE _____

A. Performance of Fundamental Strokes
   1. Forehand
      a. Grip
      b. Stance
      c. Backswing
      d. Racquet path
      e. Eye focus
      f. Contact point
      g. Wrist action
      h. Follow-through
   2. Overall rating of forehand
   3. Backhand
      a. Grip
      b. Stance
      c. Backswing
      d. Racquet path
      e. Eye focus
      f. Contact point
      g. Wrist action
      h. Follow-through
   4. Overall rating of backhand
B. Game Situations
   1. Placement and types of serves used?
   2. Player movement following the serve?
   3. Strategy in returning the serve?
   4. Court movement during rallies
      a. Behind the ball during strokes?
      b. Anticipating shots and moving in time?
      c. Returning to center court after hitting the ball?

     d. Watching the ball or the front wall during play?
     e. Moving to avoid hinders?
     f. Constantly hitting overhead shots?
  5. Ability to hit the ball when it came off the back wall
  6. Shot used to end the rally
  7. Shot hit that resulted in a setup for the opponent

C. Shot Selection

Tally the use of these shots:

1. Kill shots_____   3. Pinch shots_____   5. Passing shots_____
2. Ceiling balls_____   4. Overheads_____   6. Others _____

D. Overall Rating of Strengths and Weaknesses

4

Strategy, or Controlling the Tempo of the Game

Racquetball is a thinking person's game at all levels of play. The individual who goes on the court and simply attempts to get the racquet on the ball, hoping that it will hit the front wall, will soon be frustrated by players of lesser skill who have a game plan. There is more to the game than just hitting the ball! If you listen to spectators watching a match, you immediately become aware of this fact. You are sure to hear them offering the following bits of advice to anyone who will listen:

"Keep the ball to the backhand side."
"Slow the game down."
"You're playing his (or her) game."
"Take over center court."
"Go to the ceiling."
"Change your serve."

All of these comments indicate that there is something a player can do to control the tenor and the tempo of the game. Observation of advanced players reveals that there are several general techniques that they use to capitalize on their strengths, while simultaneously taking advantage of their opponents' weaknesses. The following five general suggestions can be applied to any style of play and to any situation which might occur during a game. If you can incorporate these suggestions into your style of play, you will increase your opportunities to take high-percentage shots while decreasing your opponent's chances.

1. Play with Confidence.   Acquire a solid working knowledge of the rules of the game (Chapter 9), the court movements, the stroke mechanics, and all the other necessary components of the game. My philosophy is that the person who has a sound knowledge of the game can better visualize and implement the skills needed to be successful. Reading and talking about racquetball can also make you a more discerning observer. Concurrently you should practice, practice, practice and play, play, play! Remember that your ability to devise and execute a game plan is directly related to the efficiency of your stroke and your accuracy in placing the ball. Obviously, if you cannot hit the ball in a preplanned direction, your strategy will be to retrieve all shots, hoping that someday your opponent will make a mistake or that you will miraculously roll the ball out. Hours of quality practice and play will give you the confidence to hit the shot needed to win those 20–20 cliff-hangers.

2. Watch the Ball at All Times.   The element that differentiates the advanced from the lower-level player is the ability to anticipate where the opponent is going to hit the ball and to get to that point, set up, and hit a high-percentage shot. This ability is a direct result of watching the ball. During a rally, the advanced player is positioned so that the opponent and the ball are always in view. When the opponent hits the ball, his or her body language and the contact point indicate both ball direction and speed, allowing the better player to move into position for the next shot *before* the ball hits the front wall. The lower-level player tends to look at the front wall throughout the rally, thereby losing sight of the ball. Consequently, following an opponent's shot, this player does not make a first move until *after* the ball has hit the front wall. This results in poor anticipation, poor court position, and poor shot selection and execution.

3. Play to Your Strengths and to Your Opponent's Weaknesses. The hours that you spend in practice sessions, lessons, and games should give you a good indication of the strong and weak points of your game. Correct assessment of this information tells you if you are a power or a control player, if your backhand will score points or get you into trouble, if you perform better in the front court or the backcourt, if your ceiling ball is worth attempting, if you have a viable "Z" serve, and so forth. This knowledge provides the basis of your game plan.

Your strategy should revolve around forcing your opponent to hit the ball into your strong zones and then using your high-percentage shots to score. To maximize your opportunities to score, you should concentrate on hitting high-percentage shots (your strengths) about 90 percent to 95 percent of the time and low-percentage shots (your weaknesses) about 5 percent to 10 percent of the time. In a twenty-one-point game you might hit the ball sixty times; three to six of your shots should be out of character, or low-percentage, shots for a given situation. These shots may be outright winners if your opponent expects you to hit a different shot, or they may keep your opponent off-balance and make your other shots more effective.

Game strategy calls for you to take advantage of your assets. The easiest way to accomplish this is to expose and exploit your opponent's liabilities. Pressure applied to these areas of an opponent's game results in weak returns and easy points.

The best way to determine the major points of weakness in an opponent's game is to observe the person playing. You can systematically analyze patterns of play by using the racquetball game analysis form presented in session 18, page 83. Chart as many games as possible, paying special attention to items B6 and B7. This analysis should assist you in determining the patterns of play and the adaptability of your opponent to changing game situations.

If you do not have the opportunity to watch an opponent play prior to your match, there are several things you can look for to quickly analyze a given player's strengths and weaknesses. Watch this player during the warm-up period. Observe both the mechanics and results of the forehand and backhand strokes. Note if there are glaring irregularities in the strokes or differences in power. If there are differences in velocity and accuracy, and the stroke looks awkward, you should develop a game plan to force your opponent to use that particular stroke.

You can also use the beginning of the game against an unknown opponent to discover weaknesses. Don't labor under the misconception that all players have a weak backhand. For many individuals, the backhand is a more natural stroke, and if you spend the whole game hitting to that side, you are in for a short and frustrating experience. Try a variety of serves and shots early in the game to determine where your opponent has problems. You may find that a ceiling ball is your best offensive weapon!

The mere process of analyzing your opponent's play will make you a more astute observer and player. If nothing else, you will at least know whether you are playing a right-handed or left-handed opponent.

4. Return to, and Control, the Center-Court Area.   The wise opponent hits shots that are as far away from you as possible, or that put you in a poor position for your return shot. To counter this strategy, you should attempt to position yourself so that you can move the shortest possible distance to return each shot. The ideal place for you to be when your opponent hits a shot is a spot equidistant from all four corners of the court. This spot is actually on the short service line in the center of the court. Because of the constantly changing situations and the ball speed and placement during any given rally, players should continually strive to come back to a position that is four to five feet behind the short service line and as close as possible to the center of the court. Remember that you must give your opponent a fair chance to see the ball and to hit the front wall on each shot. You cannot physically seize and hold the center-court area. Rather, you must use intelligent shot selection and court savvy to maintain this position. From this ideal location, you should be able to control your opponent and hit many high-percentage shots.

5. Try to Place the Ball away from Your Opponent.   This strategy is the same as the one in the old baseball adage "hit it where they ain't." In general, if your opponent is on one side of the court, hit the ball to the other side. If your opponent is in the front court, hit the ball into the backcourt area. Even when attempting to kill the ball, you should hit it away from, rather than toward, your opponent. The player who can implement this philosophy forces weak returns and causes an opponent to expend much energy. You may not score instant points with this game plan, but the effects will show up in the waning stages of the second game and in the all-important tie breaker.

These five suggestions are interrelated and should be kept in mind when preparing for any opponent. It is conceivable that you could use four different game plans or strategies for four separate matches. One strategy will not fit all game or situational circumstances. Strategies are based upon three things: (1) the previous five general suggestions, (2) situational variables as discussed in the on-court practice sessions, and (3) your opponent's style of play. The next few sections explore some of the generally accepted approaches for playing opponents with different styles of play.

PLAYING THE POWER PLAYER

The power player is the individual who strives to hit every shot as hard and as low as possible. The power player likes to "crush" the ball and enjoys the loud explosion it makes when it collides with the front wall. This player always hits a hard drive serve, even if the first attempt is a fault.

The power player appears to be in a hurry to finish the game, so your strategy should be to extend or slow down the game. Attempt to keep the ball away from the areas where it is easy to execute a hard, low shot. Try to force your opponent to contact the ball at chest height or higher. This may necessitate your using lob, half-lob, and lob Z serves to start rallies, and ceiling balls and wide-angle passes to make your opponent hit on the run, possibly resulting in a weak return.

You must guard against getting mentally caught up in the rapid pace of the game. If this happens, you will find yourself attempting to hit the ball with as much power as your opponent. This problem can be eliminated if you manage your time efficiently. When it is time for your opponent to serve, you have ten seconds after the score is called to get ready. The power player attempts to jump right into the service area and blast the ball as quickly as possible. You can force the server to wait by simply holding your racquet up in the air. The server must then wait until you lower your racquet, or the referee signals serve, to hit the ball. This will frustrate and break your opponent's rhythm.

You can also use your allotted three time-outs per game to slow the pace. If you have difficulty slowing the game down through your shot selection and enforcement of the ten-second rule, and your opponent begins to score points rapidly, call a time-out! A strategically placed time-out can break your opponent's rhythm and concentration, giving you a chance to relax and rethink your strategy. Do all that you can to avoid getting into a shooting war with the power player. If you are enticed into this type of game, you will eventually lose.

PLAYING THE CONTROL PLAYER

You will know that you are playing a control player when you seem to be running all over the court, while your opponent rarely leaves the center-court area; when you make short visitations to all four corners of the court, arriving just in time to get your racquet on the ball and hit it back to your opponent, who then directs you to another location. The control player would rather hit passing shots and ceiling balls than kill shots. This player has the ability to hit the ball accurately and to dictate the tempo of the game by getting you out of position.

Because this individual plays extremely well in the front and mid-court areas, you should attempt to force the game into the side alleys and the backcourt area. The most efficient way to accomplish this is to hit down-the-wall and wide-angle passing shots and ceiling balls. Although this appears to be a contradiction, since the control player probably has a good ceiling game, this strategy forces your opponent to attempt passing shots from a less desirable location, increasing his or her possibility of errors. Since the control player is not inherently a shooter, he or she will be forced to take a low-percentage kill shot from the backcourt to score points. Once this happens, you have taken control of the tempo of the game.

PLAYING THE RUNNER

The runner enjoys making the incredible get. When you hit passing shots or pinches that appear to be sure winners, the runner manages to retrieve the ball and keep it in play. The runner's credo is to get every ball and to force you to work hard for every point or side-out. The runner is accustomed to this style of play and would rather attempt to shoot while running than while standing still. This player scores easy points when an opponent has relaxed, thinking that the last shot was a sure winner, only to see the ball returned to an area that is out of reach.

The runner anticipates extremely well and moves to retrieve before you hit your shot. Strategically you should attempt to slow the runner to a walk or a standing position. Instead of hitting to the seemingly open areas of the court, try to hit many of your shots right at or behind the runner. The runner is usually not a particularly good shooter, so you should try to keep him or her out of the frontcourt area and force them to try to score from the backcourt.

You can use your time-outs and your ten seconds between serves to slow the momentum and to make the runner think rather than react. If you can slow this individual down and force the game to be decided on the basis of skill rather than fitness, you will control the tempo of the game to your advantage.

CONTROLLING THE TEMPO IN DOUBLES

Doubles is the only game in racquetball in which there are more participants (four), than officials (three). However, the court size for doubles is the same as for singles. Therefore, smooth, uninterrupted play requires the participants to coordinate their movements and to exercise their best court courtesy and sporting manners.

Given the speed of the ball and the inherent dangers associated with racquetball, why would anyone want to play doubles? The game does offer several benefits not found in singles. A less skilled player can compete on an equal basis with higher level players because of the emphasis on teamwork. A team of players who are less skilled can be very competitive with advanced level players who do not function well as a team. Intelligent use of court positioning and shot selection can compensate for individual movement and skill weaknesses. The application of a game plan that strategically emphasizes strengths while hiding liabilities can place the opposition at a disadvantage and result in one team controlling the tempo of play.

Selection of a doubles partner is the first step toward the development of a successful team. Since communication is such a critical element in team play, it is important that teammates be compatible. To improve, partners must communicate before, during, and after games.

Before the game begins, you must prepare a plan designed to control the tempo of play. During the game, you have to talk constantly with your partner to determine who is going to take each shot. You have to let your partner know if you are going to cover certain areas of the court and if you are going to back him or her up on a given shot. If your pregame plan does not work as well as you anticipated, you may have to change your strategy during the match. Time-outs and the period between serves can be used to discuss a change in service strategy, shot placement, and playing position.

Communication must continue after both a win and a loss, if improvement in team play is to occur. Following the match, you must be open enough to discuss your successes and failures and to make changes where necessary. Good doubles teams spend many hours together practicing on consistency of play and experimenting with new strategies and techniques. If you can find a partner who can interact with you both on and off the court, and if that person happens to be left-handed and you to be right-handed, you are on your way to successful doubles play.

Once your team has been formed, consideration should be given to how you can control the tempo of play in a given match. The skill needed to dictate the way in which the game is played depends on your approach to doubles play, or your strategy, and the type of formation you decide to use. The rest of this chapter focuses on some of the more widely accepted approaches to doubles play.

PLAYING TO THE WEAKER OPPONENT

No two players are exactly equal in ability, so one of your opponents will be a much stronger player than the other. Most of your shots should be directed to the weaker player. This increases the possibility of a weak return or an outright error. When most of the play is directed to one player, the partner begins to get frustrated and moves out of position in order to get involved in the game. When the stronger player moves into the territory of his or her partner, this increases the congestion in that area of the court and leaves other areas open. At this moment a well-placed passing shot to the strong side becomes a winner.

SERVING DEFENSIVELY

In doubles there are two people receiving the serve, making it difficult to score an outright winner. The drive serve isn't used as frequently in doubles, because court coverage allows the opposition more time to set up and shoot the return. In many cases, the drive serve freezes the serving team inside the service area and doesn't allow them the time to get into appropriate court position for the next shot.

The objective of the serve should be to keep the opponents in the backcourt area while the serving team gains control of the front court. Lob serves and lob "Z" serves are particularly effective in providing the serving team with the time needed to gain correct court position for the ensuing rally.

The serve should usually be directed to the weaker opponent. If you are playing against a right-handed and left-handed team, the ideal serve would end up in the center-court area, causing confusion and forcing each player to hit a backhand stroke in order to return the ball.

Following the serve, both partners should move to a position approximately four feet behind the short service line and away from the sidewall. If a player gets trapped on a sidewall, this effectively cuts down the amount of court space the team can cover and also increases the chances of getting hit with the ball when it is returned by either the partner or the opposition.

CONTROLLING THE FRONT-COURT AREA

The impact of front-court position is much greater in doubles than it is in singles. As in singles play, your opportunities to score multiply as you move into the middle to front-court area. The team that remains in the backcourt area discovers that it is difficult to see the ball during a rally and that there are fewer shooting lanes because of the court congestion. Conversely the team in the front is able to see the ball well and has a variety of shot options in any given situation.

The flow of play in a doubles match should resemble that of a singles match. Following each stroke, one team should rotate into position to hit the next shot, while the other team should be moving into advantageous front-court positions for the ensuing shot. The rallies and court movement can be very smooth if both teams obey the traffic patterns and allow the team receiving a shot to move into the front-court position.

Successful teams are able to keep their opponents in the back-court during most of the rallies. This is accomplished by hitting wide-angle passes, down-the-wall passes, and ceiling balls. It is also a good policy to cut the ball off and hit fly kills, pinch shots, and half volleys, in order to keep the ball in the front court and your opponents in the backcourt. These particular shots are also the most effective means of scoring points in doubles.

The doubles team that communicates well and fully understands the general strategy of play has two of the three essential elements needed for success. The third element is a play formation that matches the personality of your team and your style of play. The chosen formation will distribute court coverage to each player based upon individual strengths and weaknesses. An understanding of player responsibilities allows the team to adapt to the changing situations of the game and return to positions of strength. Doubles teams usually select one of the four following formations to begin play.

USING SIDE-BY-SIDE FORMATION

This formation is widely used by beginning teams and by those teams composed of players who have not practiced together. The court is divided in half, and each player becomes responsible for covering his or her area from the front wall to the back wall (Figure 4-1). With this setup, the center part of the court is actually a free zone, and the person with the most efficient shot should return balls hit into that area. If the team is composed of two right-handed players, the player on the left should have the best backhand and should take the major responsibility for returns from the free zone. The team can then use a forehand stroke on shots taken from the center-court area. The complementary player on the right side should have a very strong forehand and the quickness to cover the front-court area.

When the team is composed of a left-handed and a right-handed player, the coverage is arranged so that both players can hit forehand strokes. The free zone should be covered by the player who has the best backhand. Before the match, the team should decide who is going to take the shots from the free zone.

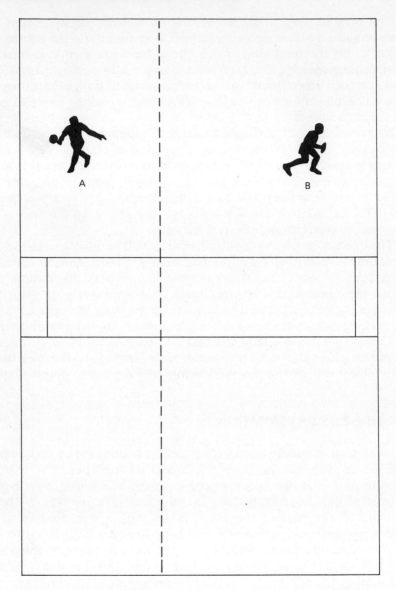

FIGURE 4-1   The side-by-side formation. Player B is responsible for shots in the center-court area

USING THE "I" FORMATION

With the "I" formation (or Front-and-Back) the players are arranged so that one is in the center of the front-court area and the other is in the center of the backcourt area (Figure 4-2). In the past this formation was used when one player had a good ceiling ball and was a good

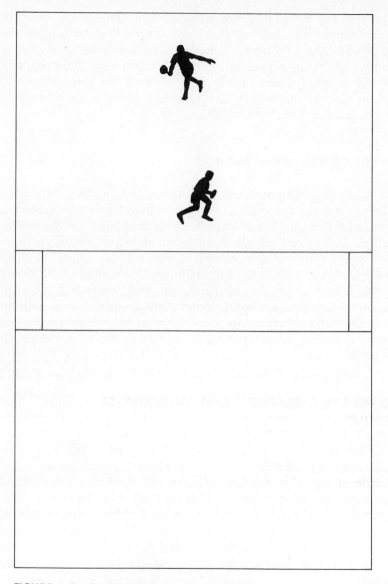

FIGURE 4-2   Setting up in the "I" formation

shooter, and the partner was quick and willing to dive and retrieve shots in the front court. This formation gives the illusion of effectiveness when in reality it has many weaknesses and is therefore used infrequently.

A good opposing team can easily isolate the front-court player by occupying the side alleys. They can then force the backcourt player to run from side to side to return passing shots. In essence they are then competing against a one-person team. The front-court player gets frustrated from lack of play, and the backcourt player gets fatigued and begins to hit poor returns. Another weakness of this system is that the front player tends to get in the way. This player often physically screens a shot, making it difficult for the partner to see, and when the partner can return the shot, there is an increased possibility of hitting the front-court player.

USING THE COMBINATION METHOD

Teams using this approach start out in a side-by-side or "I" formation and change during the rallies. The position of the ball and the players dictates whether the team uses a front-and-back or a side-by-side formation. When one player on a team moves to return a shot, the partner must move into position to cover open areas. During the game each player has to assume the roles of retriever, shooter, and defensive player on both the forehand and backhand sides of the court. Obviously this system is used more frequently by well-skilled individuals who communicate well. Players who choose to use a combination formation must have more than adequate skills in all aspects of the game.

USING THE THREE-QUARTERS–AND–ONE-QUARTER FORMATION

This is the old "I'll take everything" formation. One player covers three-quarters of the court, and the partner concentrates on the forehand side of the front quarter (Figure 4-3). When a team has one dominant player, it may opt for this style of play. The decision to use this system can be made before the match, or the dominant player can subtlely take over more and more territory as the game progresses. The more competitive the situation, and the greater the difference in skill levels of the teammates, the more likely you are to see this formation.

There are many weaknesses in this style of play. The most obvious is that one person is playing against two opponents. Court coverage is more difficult, fatigue eventually sets in, and the team suffers.

Philosophically, relegating one player to a small section of the court and to a small role in the total game is contrary to the concept of team play. The idea of the game is to share equally in the participation, to complement each other's skill, and to engage jointly in the contest for the improvement of play and the enjoyment it brings. The

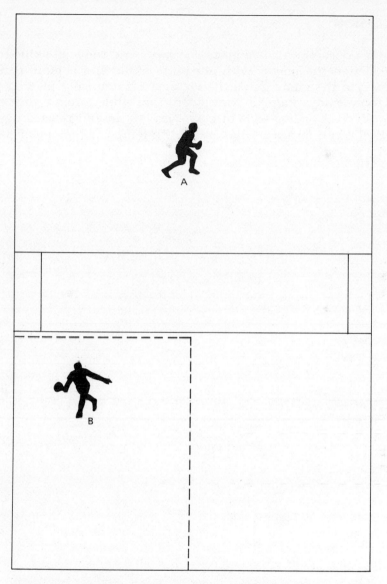

FIGURE 4-3 Three-quarters—and—one-quarter formation. Player A returns almost every shot, while Player B covers a small area of the court.

player who covers one-fourth of the court quickly loses the motivation to play and does not have the opportunity to develop and improve the skills needed to complement his or her partner. Therefore the player who needs the most work on game skills does not improve with this system. It is difficult to find a player who will agree to participate in this type of system, and as a result, it is rarely seen.

CONCLUSION

The game does not always go to the swift and the well-skilled individual. Often the player with adequate skills and a more cerebral approach to the game gains the victory. Strategically placing your shots to take advantage of your strengths, while forcing your opponent out of his or her style of play, can be fun and rewarding. The player who can successfully control the tempo of play emerges the victor!

5

A Different View of the Hinder Rule: Beware of the Wheel

Ecchymosis runs rampant in most racquetball clubs. It strikes both the novice and the professional player. It can occur in isolated areas of the body or in epidemic proportions on various body segments. Depending upon your point of view, it can be the mark of distinction signifying that you have arrived in the world of racquetball or it can be the reason that you have moved to a more humane sport such as tennis.

You may have already figured out that ecchymosis is the welt or "wheel" that is left after a racquetball has been peeled off or dug out of your body following a vigorous stroke by an opponent. *Stedman's Medical Dictionary* defines ecchymosis as "a purplish patch caused by extravasation of blood into the skin; a black and blue mark." Racquetball players are aware of the fact that this mark from a ball becomes not only purple, black, and blue but also every other color of the rainbow as it goes through the healing process and finally disappears. Not only is this wheel colorful, but it also hurts—a great deal!

The wheel, although aesthetically displeasing and painful, can be an aid to those who are interested in rating their opposition. Intricate racquetball rating scales have been developed to classify players

---

Stedman's Medical Dictionary, 21st ed. (Baltimore: The Williams and Wilkins Company, 1966), p. 498.

This chapter is taken from James Sylvis, "A Different View of the Hinder Rule: Beware of the Wheel," *National Racquetball Magazine*, vol. 10, no. 1 (January 1981), pp. 44–46.

into Novice, C, B, and A categories. Utilization of these scales requires the rater to observe a player for several hours in a competitive situation. This is time-consuming and frequently inaccurate. I believe you can rank players accurately and quickly according to the number and anatomical locations of their wheels. Beginning players have more wheels per capita, and they are usually found on the upper parts of their bodies. As players improve and begin to hit the ball harder and closer to the floor, the number and location of their wheels is lower. No intelligent human would stand in front of one of Marty Hogan's 142 mile-per-hour bullets!

The player who understands and implements the rules on hinders will not get wheeled. The rule book clearly defines a hinder as any unintentional interference that prevents an opponent from having a fair chance to see or to return the ball. It further states that it is an *avoidable* hinder if, intentionally or unintentionally, (1) a player does not move sufficiently to allow an opponent a shot, (2) a player moves into a position that blocks an opponent's attempt to return the ball, (3) a player moves into the ball and is struck by it after an opponent has played it, and (4) a player moves so close to an opponent that he or she does not have a free, unimpeded swing. A hinder results in a replay, and an avoidable hinder causes an automatic loss of serve or a point. These hinders, along with causing ill feelings and arguments, are also all wheel-makers.

Avoidable hinders usually occur because players do not understand or implement the rules. Players make what they feel are intelligent moves in order to take away opponents' options on given shots. Consider the following situations:

1. Player A is ready to hit a perfect shot on which an easy point can be scored. As the shot is hit, Player B steps in front of, and is hit by, the ball (Figure 5-1).

2. Player A is in perfect position to hit one of several possible shots such as a straight-in-kill, a down-the-line pass, a cross-court pass, or a reverse pinch, when Player B moves into the shooting lanes and eliminates several of these options. This forces Player A to hit an easily anticipated shot (Figure 5-2).

3. Player A is ready to hit a given shot and Player B moves so close to Player A that the hitter feels intimidated and is forced to change the shot.

To take these shots out of the repertoire of the well-wheeled player, there must be a good referee for every game and a course in sportsmanship. (And you can hope your opponent didn't take Charlie Brumfield too seriously in his November 1980, *National Racquetball Magazine* article on "playing it close".) To avoid a player's getting wheels, the elimination of hinders must become an automatic part of

FIGURE 5-1   One player steps in front of the other and gets hit by the shot

the game for all players. A good guideline in this endeavor is to attempt to give an opponent a clear shot from the racquet face to both corners of the front wall on all shots (Figure 5-3). To stay out of this triangular area while an opponent is hitting the ball, and thus avoid hinders and wheels, a player must be able to see the opponent when the ball is hit.

Watching the ball is another antiwheel measure. In every sport which calls for manipulation of an object, it is essential to keep an eye on the object in order to hit it, kick it, strike it, and so forth. In racquetball it is also very important to watch the ball *after* hitting it. Unfortunately many racquetball players (usually those with the most wheels) do not watch the ball following their strokes. They hit the ball and then back up into the center of the court with their eyes riveted

FIGURE 5-2   Forcing your opponent to shoot around you

on the front wall and every muscle in their body tensed in anticipation of the impending collision. The ball ricochets around the walls to a position that is usually behind them. Opponents have eyes fixed on the ball in preparation for the hit and never see the other player. As a result of not visually tracking the ball, the initial hitter usually winds up unintentionally planted in the shooting lane (Figures 5-1 and 5-2). The result—a giant wheel! This could be avoided by simply watching the ball.

FIGURE 5-3   Correctly watching the opponent while giving him or her a clear shot to the front wall

To become adept at watching the ball, players must force them-selves to do it in warm-up and game situations, wearing eyeguards, of course. They can also set up drills in which they serve the ball to another person, move to the appropriate position on the court (feet on one side of the triangle formed by the opponents' racquet face and both corners of the front wall), take a half- or a quarter-turn, and glance over their shoulders at opponents (Figure 5-3). Players should never turn and fully face opponents, as this is a very vulnerable position. Anyone who has a wheel on the front part of the body should be immediately placed at the bottom of the rating scale. These drills should be repeated with two- and three-hit rallies until a player feels comfortable moving into position and watching the ball. The use of eyeguards makes this a safe and easily learned skill.

Visual tracking of the ball, besides reducing wheels, leads to better anticipation, correct court position and movement, and advanced stroking patterns. The player who has perfected these skills is well on the way to the top of the ladder and to the bottom of the Sylvis Ecchymosis Rating Scale.

The next time that strangers or unranked players challenge you to a friendly game, and you want to assure yourself of an enjoyable afternoon, apply the ecchymosis rating scale before you accept. Look them over in the locker room and check their wheels. If it appears that someone has taken a ball on a rope and maliciously beaten one of these players about the arms, back, buttocks, and legs, you should politely decline to play and suggest that the person take lessons.

Never play an individual who is wearing protective clothing, for instance, a sweat suit from neck to toe. These individuals have decided that it is easier to be well padded than it is to examine and change their games. Under all of that clothing, you can bet that ecchymosis lurks. If, on the other hand, an individual has only one or two wheels, and they are on the lower and upper leg, you can probably rest assured that the games will go smoothly and not be interrupted by constant cries of "Ouch" and "Hinder."

6

Problems Encountered by the Former Tennis Player

Racquetball has been widely promoted as a game that is easily learned and one which offers players quick success and enjoyment. This message has not been lost on the tennis players of America. They have flocked to racquetball clubs, hoping that their tennis skills could be readily adapted to the game of racquetball. In most cases they find that the transition is not so smooth.

Interested friends and teaching pros quickly become frustrated in their attempts to adapt tennis behaviors to a *completely* different game—racquetball. These frustrations, and the players' difficulties, arise from something which C.L. Hull termed *proactive inhibition* (a form of negative transfer). This phenomenon occurs when a previously learned skill interferes with the acquisition of a similar skill attempted at a later date. In this case, tennis has a deleterious effect on the performance of essential racquetball skills. If we, as instructors and players, hope to save our hair and our friends, we must deal with the problems quickly and effectively.

Transformation of a tennis player to a racquetball enthusiast entails a progressive instructional program based upon diagnostic teaching. The realization that proactive inhibition does occur makes observation and critical analysis crucial to the teaching and learning process. Observation of tennis-racquetball players indicates that

This chapter is taken from James Sylvis, "The Grand Conversion from Tennis to Racquetball," *National Racquetball Magazine,* vol. 10, no. 2 (February 1981), pp. 36–37.

their difficulties fall into two general categories: (1) the mechanics of stroke execution, and (2) court movement. An in-depth analysis of these two areas reveals several specific movement patterns inherent in tennis players that interfere with the acquisition of racquetball skills.

The first general area of concern centers around stroke execution. A subskill analysis of both the tennis and the racquetball forehand stroke (the backhand exhibits similar elements and problems) reveals that they are composed of the same basic elements. Each stroke has the following components:

1. Grip
2. Footwork (stance)
3. Backswing
4. Racquet path (movement)
5. Eye focus
6. Contact point
7. Body movement
8. Wrist snap (involvement)
9. Follow-through

It is in the execution of these elements that the strokes differ. The major interference occurs in elements (3) backswing, (4) racquet path, (6) contact point, (8) wrist action, and (9) follow-through. Therefore, in order to eliminate the effects of proactive inhibition, we must identify the differences in each element and then attempt to change them.

The tennis player's problems begin with the backswing. In moving from the ready position to the backswing, the racquet is brought almost straight back and in line with the flight of the ball. The ensuing racquet position is usually low, with the arm and racquet relatively straight and pointing directly backward (Figure 6-1). This racquet position allows a player to hit the ball up and over the net. Since this is not the objective in racquetball, the backswing is the first thing that must be changed. The traditional description of the racquetball backswing places the elbow at a height at least equal to the shoulder, with the forearm perpendicular to the upper arm and the racquet cocked toward the head (Figure 6-2). The racquet must be brought to a higher position to build racquet speed and to allow the player to hit down on the ball to produce a low flight. This position is alien to the tennis player and must be practiced so that it becomes an automatic movement.

The path the racquet follows in going from the backswing to the

FIGURE 6-1 The low, straight-arm tennis backswing

contact point is critical to the correct racquetball stroking pattern. The tennis player who has achieved a good racquetball backswing often initiates the stroke by dropping the arm down to the low straight position, with the racquet pointing directly backward (Figure 6-1). This forces him or her to swing from the shoulder in the familiar tennis style. The racquetball swing begins with the elbow and handle butt leading, as the racquet is pulled toward the ball and the contact point. The racquet arm remains bent and the wrist cocked until just prior to contact, at which time the arm is straightened and the wrist is vigorously flexed to create racquet speed and force (Fig-

FIGURE 6-2 The high racquetball backswing

FIGURE 6-3   The initiation of the swing, leading with the elbow and the racquet handle

FIGURE 6-4   Moving from the backswing to the contact point. Just prior to contact the arm gets to a straight position, and the wrist remains flexed and ready to apply force. The ball is contacted low, near the ankle.

ures 6-3 and 6-4). There has been some success in simulating the correct racquet path by asking the player to imagine pulling a bell rope from the high backswing to the contact point. This simulation provides a feel for the bent-to-straight-arm position.

The next problem that must be tackled is the contact point. The tennis player has a mental set to contact the ball at the peak of its flight (Figure 6-5). This causes two problems; first, the return shot is always high on the front wall; and second, the player constantly moves forward in order to hit the ball at its highest point. In contrast, the racquetball player tries to contact the ball at its lowest point in flight (Figure 6-4). Therefore, on returns in which the tennis player is moving forward, the racquetball player is moving backward to the hitting position. The following drills (along with constant verbal feedback from a friend) can help to eliminate this problem. First, stand in a forehand stroking position, drop the ball from mid-thigh, and attempt to hit it before it hits the floor. Second, drop the ball, allow it to bounce, and then attempt to hit it after it has peaked and is headed for the floor. Third, one player hits the ball off the front wall

FIGURE 6-5   The tennis player hits the ball at the peak of its flight, before it has a chance to drop to a low point.

at about waist height while the other player attempts to move into a hitting position for contacting the ball at its lowest point. These three drills, along with constant verbal feedback, can help to change the tennis player's mental set.

Wrist action and follow-through are the two elements which differentiate the racquetball stroke from the tennis stroke and give each its character. The tennis player has been instructed to maintain a straight arm and wrist position throughout the swing and to finish with the racquet pointing forward toward the top of the opposite fence (Figure 6-6). In contrast, the racquetball player gets to the contact point with the wrist carrying the racquet arm across the body, to end pointing toward the wall behind him or her (Figure 6-7). The wrist action is critical to the development of power and consistency in the stroke and can be developed through simulated movements. One simulation has the player in a kneeling position with the racquet held at approximately the mid-body position. From this setup, the ball is dropped, and the player attempts to hit it using only the wrist snap. During play or drills the player should always check the finishing position of each swing to determine if the racquet is facing the opposite wall. This is the best indication that the wrist is involved in the stroke.

The previous suggestions can be helpful in changing the mechanics of players' strokes, but they do little for their court movement or positioning. This is another aspect of the tennis game that interferes with success in racquetball. The tennis player is accustomed to playing the base line and watching the opponent hit the

FIGURE 6-6   The tennis player follows through with the racquet pointing straight ahead. There is little or no wrist involvement.

FIGURE 6-7   The racquetball player explodes with the wrist at contact and finishes the swing pointing the racquet at the wall behind him or her.

ball at him or her. A tennis player never has to turn and track a ball originating from a point behind him or her. The majority of the movements a tennis player makes are from side to side at the baseline or in a diagonally forward direction, hardly ever diagonally backward. Racquetball is composed of movements in all directions. More importantly, the players are constantly moving forward to take over the center-court position and then diagonally backward to hit the next shot. The tennis-racquetball player cannot be content to play the baseline, but must move up after every shot and must learn to visually track balls being hit from behind him or her. Eyeguards and a great deal of situational practice can enhance the tennis-racquetball player's court coverage. The Star Drill (session 1) and the practice tasks in sessions 6 and 7 can also help to break detrimental habits.

Although racquetball is easily learned, it can be both frustrating and challenging to an athlete from another sport. The problems are especially acute for a tennis player because of the similarities in the activities. It takes an awareness of the differences in the games and a conscious effort on the part of the player to overcome the effects of proactive inhibition. If one is successful in this endeavour, racquetball can become an enjoyable leisure-time activity.

7

Exercises
for Racquetball

Racquetball is an exciting, action-filled game requiring a high degree of physically demanding activity. One of the best ways to improve your game, while at the same time minimizing your risk of injury, is to augment the time you spend on the court with a well-planned conditioning program. Attaining and maintaining a high level of physical fitness is easy if you spend a few minutes each day doing endurance, flexibility, and muscle-strengthening exercises.

Endurance for racquetball is best developed by running slow, long distances during the "off season," developing a solid aerobic base, and gradually mixing in sprints and footwork drills as you approach the playing season. These short sprints and drills help to develop the speed, explosiveness, and agility necessary on the court.

WARM-UP

An important part of any racquetball program is the warm-up. Most people, it seems, have heard that proper warm-up may improve athletic performance and help minimize injury, but very few people understand what a proper warm-up really is, what it does, or what it is composed of.

A warm-up is a period of activity that gradually takes the body from a resting state to a level of optimal working condition, ready for intense physical work. An adequate warm-up helps to increase your

This chapter was contributed by Tom Haney of the Village Glen Tennis and Fitness Club, Williamsville, New York.

endurance, speed, and strength and even improves a player's overall physical condition. The likelihood of tears and other injuries to the muscles and connective tissue is also greatly reduced by properly warming up.

But what exactly constitutes a proper warm-up? To be most effective, a warm-up should include activities that elevate body temperature, like jogging, walking, or bicycling (perhaps one to five minutes). This is followed by a series of dynamic "swinging" exercises such as jumping jacks, neck curls, arm circles, and toe touching. Once the muscles are warmed, they should be carefully stretched through slow, static, stretching exercises. The critical factor in a static stretch is to apply gentle pressure until tightness occurs and then to hold the position for a period of fifteen to sixty seconds (see the section on flexibility for specific instructions and exercises, pgs. 115–18).

The final stages of a warm-up center around the movements specific to racquetball. Begin to hit slowly. Start near the short service line, and as you feel comfortable, gradually move back toward the back wall. Forehands, backhands, overheads, serves, and pinch shots should all be used. The basic footwork used during a game should also be practiced at gradually increasing speeds. Once this regimen is completed, you are ready to play.

There are many excellent exercises that have been suggested for use during warm-up and cool-down phases of racquetball. You can select some of the dynamic exercises in this chapter to start your warm-up period and follow these with the flexibility exercises.

DYNAMIC STRETCHING EXERCISES

NECK ROTATIONS   Turn your head to the right through a full range of movement, then repeat rotation to the left. Move slowly and stretch gently. Repeat five times to each side.

NECK CIRCLES   Make full circles with your head, attempting to touch your chin to your chest and your ears to your shoulders as you make the circles. Do five clockwise revolutions, then five counterclockwise revolutions.

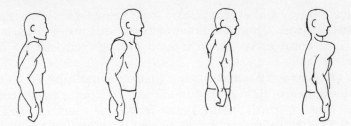

SHOULDER SHRUGS Lift your shoulders up toward your ears, then roll them forward. Repeat these forward rotations five or more times. Then lift your shoulders toward your ears and rotate them backward. Repeat these backward rotations five or more times.

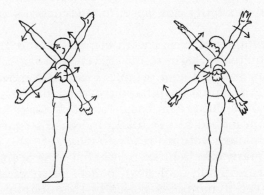

ARM CIRCLES (Forward and Backward) Swing arms in circular motion from your shoulders. Gradually increase the size of the circles until you reach a full arm swinging. Repeat in opposite direction.

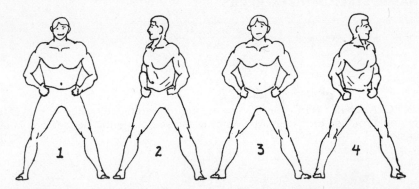

TRUNK TWISTER Stand with your feet shoulder-width apart and your hands on your hips. Twist trunk to the right as far as is comfortably possibly; recoil to the other direction as far as comfortably possible. Do these twists five or more times to each side. Never force this exercise; keep it rhythmic and gentle.

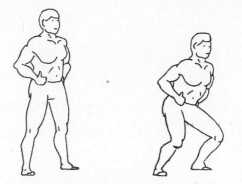

KNEE BENDS   Stand erect with your feet about shoulder-width apart. Bend your knees slowly until the angle formed between your upper and lower leg is about ninety degrees. Return to standing position, and repeat five or more times.

FLEXIBILITY

Flexibility is an important physical component for anyone playing racquetball. Adequate flexibility not only allows you to maneuver better on the court, but loose, pliable muscles are much less susceptible to strains and tears. Flexibility is best developed by static stretching. This method of stretching is designed to coax, not force, muscles to relax and lengthen. The first step in stretching is to assume a bodily position that allows you to isolate the muscles to be stretched (see the following illustrations). Then you gently apply pressure until you feel tightness or a gentle stretching. Maintain this position for a period of ten seconds or more (as much as sixty seconds is not inappropriate for very tight muscles), while constantly trying to increase the degree of relaxation in the muscles being stretched. This stretching process should include all of the major muscle groups, particularly those involved in racquetball such as the muscles of the legs, lower back, and shoulders.

The following flexibility exercises can be used as part of the general warm-up session or during the cool-down period following a vigorous match.

SINGLE LEG TUCK   Lie flat on the ground. Bring one knee up toward your chest. Grab your leg just below the knee, and gently pull the knee toward your chest. Hold this position for ten seconds or longer, then repeat the procedure with the other leg.

DOUBLE LEG TUCK   Start by lying flat on the ground. Bring both knees up toward your chest. With your arms, grab both legs just below the knees, and gently pull them toward your chest. Hold this position for ten seconds or longer.

SINGLE-LEG SIT AND REACH   Sit with the sole of one foot on the inside of the opposite thigh. Use your arms to gently pull your head toward your knee. Hold the stretch for ten seconds or more. Reverse legs and repeat.

GROIN STRETCH   Sit with the soles of your feet together. Press knees apart with elbows until you feel a stretch on the inner thigh area. Hold stretched position for ten seconds or more.

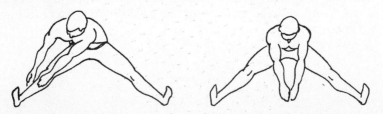

WIDE STRADDLE LEG STRETCH   Sit in a straddle position and straighten back. Using your arms for assistance, slowly bring your head as close as possible to your right knee. Hold stretch for at least ten seconds. Repeat stretch to left side. Now attempt to bring your chin to the floor between your legs. Hold stretch for ten seconds or more.

THIGH STRETCH   Lie on your left side, bend your right leg, and grab your ankle with your right hand. By gently pulling your right heel toward your head, you will experience a stretch in your thigh. Hold the stretch position for ten seconds or longer, then repeat the process on the other side.

HEAD TO KNEES   Seated with your legs together, bend forward bringing your head toward your knees. Hold stretch for ten seconds or more.

SEATED TORSO TWIST   Sit with your left leg straight and your right leg bent at the knee so that your foot rests flat on the floor next to your left knee. Turn your head, shoulders, and torso at the right until you can place your left elbow on the outside of your right knee. Apply gentle pressure with your elbow until you experience a stretch in your lower back or abdomen. Hold the position for ten seconds or more, then reverse leg positions and repeat twist to opposite side.

CALF STRETCH   Stand approximately three feet away from a wall. Step forward with one foot and brace yourself against the wall with your hands. Keep your front leg bent and your rear leg straight. While keeping the heel of your rear leg firmly on the ground, lean forward until you experience a stretch in the lower part of your straight leg. Hold the stretch for ten seconds or longer, then repeat the procedure with the other leg. *NOTE:* A slight bend in the back knee will improve the stretch on the *lower* calf area.

CHEST STRETCH　Sit or stand up straight. Interlace your fingers behind your head, and gently push your elbows back as far as possible. Hold the stretch for ten seconds or longer.

ARM AND SHOULDER STRETCH　With arms extended overhead and palms together, stretch your arms upward and slightly backward. Hold the stretch for ten seconds or longer.

TRICEP AND SHOULDER STRETCH　With your arms over your head, hold the elbow of one arm with the hand of the other arm. Gently pull the elbow behind your head. Hold the stretch for at least ten seconds, then repeat with the other side.

MUSCULAR STRENGTH

Muscular strength is an often-overlooked element in the conditioning of a racquetball player, but it is very important. Your muscular condition plays a significant role in how quickly you move on the court and how hard you hit the ball. Muscular strength is also a key element to the stability of various joints, particularly those joints that are most susceptible to injury: knees, shoulders, elbows, and wrists.

To develop muscular fitness, you must use some form of overload training. That is, you must apply resistance to the muscles in a progressive, systematic manner. For those who are highly motivated and deeply devoted to the game, many special programs and intricate devices are available. For most recreational players, however, a regular program of calisthenics, such as push-ups, pull-ups, and knee bends, goes a long way toward improving muscle tone. There are some special exercises you can do for the muscles specific to racquetball (see the following illustrations). These exercises should be performed two or three times each week, for about ten to twenty repetitions each. Once an exercise becomes relatively easy, increase the resistance slightly. The key to this program is consistency, regularity, and progression.

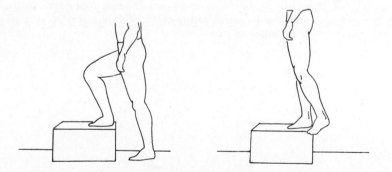

BENCH STEPPING   Stand facing the bench. Place one foot on top of the bench, and then the other (so that you are standing on the bench). Put one foot back on the floor, and then the other. Repeat this process as often as desired, alternating lead foot periodically. As your conditioning improves, increase the duration and/or the speed of this exercise.

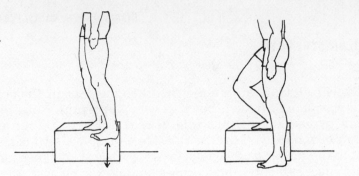

LATERAL BENCH STEPPING   Stand with your right side to the bench and your right foot on the bench. Using only the strength of your right leg, stand on the bench. Keeping your left leg straight, lower yourself until your heel touches the ground. Keep your right foot flat on the bench, and do not push off the floor with your left foot or leg. Do this exercise slowly as many times as necessary, then repeat the process with your left leg on the bench.

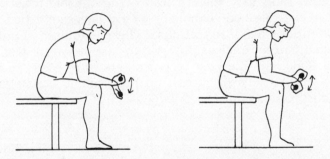

WRIST CURLS   Sit with your forearms resting on your thighs. Hold a weight in your hand with your palm up. Lower the weight by extending your wrist and allowing the weight to roll out to your fingertips. Now close your hand and flex your wrist. Do this exercise as often as necessary, then repeat the process with your palms facing down. *NOTE:* Be sure to keep your forearms firmly on your thighs and be sure to get as much movement of your wrists as possible.

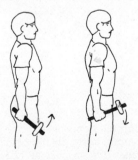

RADIAL DEVIATION   Hold a bar weight near one end so that the extra length extends from the thumb side of your hand. Raise and lower the weight by moving only your wrist, pulling your thumb up toward your elbow and back down.

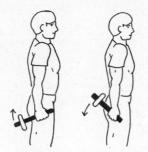

ULNAR DEVIATION Hold a bar weight near one end so that the extra length extends from the little-finger side of your hand. Raise and lower the weight by moving your wrist, so that the little finger is pulled up toward your elbow and back down.

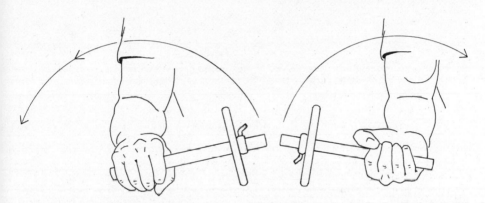

PRONATION AND SUPINATION Hold a bar weight at one end, with your palm down and the extra length extending from the thumb side of your hand. Turn your hand over to a palm up position, and then return to palm-down position.

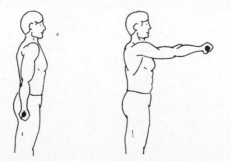

FORWARD RAISE Hold a weight at your side, then raise it to a position in front of and slightly higher than your shoulder. Return to starting position and repeat. Do the exercise slowly.

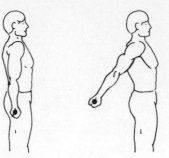

BACKWARD RAISE   Hold a weight at your side, then push it straight back as high as possible without bending at the waist. Return to starting position and repeat.

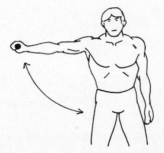

LATERAL RAISE   Hold a weight at your side, then raise it to a position out to the side and slightly above shoulder height. Return. Do this exercise slowly.

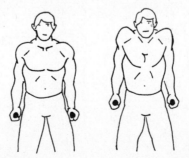

WEIGHTED SHOULDER SHRUGS   Hold a weight in each hand, then raise your shoulders up toward your ears (as high as possible). Lower and repeat.

SHOULDER PRESS Hold a weight at shoulder height, then push the weight straight up to arm's length. Lower and repeat.

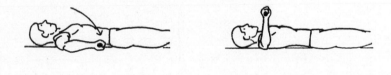

SHOULDER ROTATION Lie on your back with a weight in your hand. Bring your elbow to shoulder height, and bend elbow to ninety degrees. Starting with your palm down, rotate your arm until reaching a palms-up position. Return to start and repeat.

ABDOMINAL TIGHTENING Lie on your back on the floor. Keep your knees bent and your feet flat on the floor. Raise your head and shoulders off the floor, and exhale as you come up. Once your shoulders have left the floor, push your rib cage down toward your hips. Inhale as you return to flat position, and repeat.

KNEES TO CHEST Lie on your back with your hands under your buttocks. Bend your knees and bring them up to your chest, then extend them until they are almost straight and almost touching the ground. Now bring your knees back up to your chest. Repeat this exercise five or more times. *NOTE:* For those with weak abdominal muscles, do the exercise with the knees continually bent and allow the feet to touch the floor between each repetition.

ADVANCED

ELBOW TO OPPOSITE KNEE Lie on your back with knees bent and feet flat on the floor. Keep your hands behind your neck. Lift your right knee and your left elbow at the same time until they meet at mid-torso. Return to starting position, then repeat with opposite elbow and knee. Try to do this exercise at least five times to each side.

ABDOMINAL TIGHTENING WITH TWISTS   Lie on your back with your knees bent and your hands behind your neck. Raise your head and shoulders off of the floor, then twist your torso (from the waist) from side to side. Repeat five times or more to each side.

SEATED KNEE TO CHEST   Sit with your arms to your side, palms flat on the floor, for support. Bring your knees to your chest (feet off floor). Extend legs and torso until each is about one foot from the floor. Repeat five or more times.

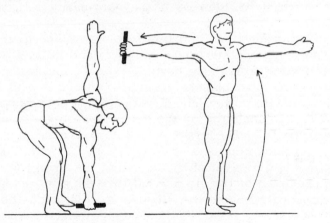

WEIGHTED TORSO BEND AND TWIST   Start by standing erect with your arms extended to the side at shoulder height. Hold a weight in your right hand. Bend over at the waist, bending the legs slightly, until the weight in your right hand touches your left foot. Return to a standing position, and twist your torso to the right. Repeat as required, then place weight in left hand and reverse the entire process. Repeat.

DEVELOPMENT OF STROKE POWER

Involvement in sport can provide the participant with many opportunities for peak experiences—the crack of the bat and the great catch in baseball, the swish in basketball, the ace in tennis, and the strategic victory in all sports.[7] In racquetball, one of these moments occurs when the ball jumps off the racquet face and explodes into the front wall. This aspect of the game has been glamorized by the power play of the touring pros, as exemplified by the 142-mile-per-hour shots of Marty Hogan. Aspiring players of both sexes at all levels of play often wonder why they can't hit the ball harder.

The answer to this question is multifaceted. The generation of power at the point of impact is determined by a variety of factors. The mechanics and efficiency of the stroke and the player's ability to get into the correct position to hit the shot are certainly instrumental factors. Another element of critical importance to racquet-head speed and force is muscular strength. Unfortunately, the training program adopted by most racquetball players focuses on the development of flexibility, aerobic capacity, and skill proficiency. Exercises devoted to the improvement of muscular strength and endurance are usually forgotten while the player does the obligatory stretching prior to entering the court to practice or play. This often-overlooked and essential aspect of basic physical fitness could determine if a player's shots are outright winners or if they are easily returned by an opponent.

Muscular strength is important to successful performance for a variety of reasons. It plays a role in injury and fatigue prevention, and is therefore of value in the development of consistency of performance. However, most players are more concerned with its role in hitting the ball with power. The development of power is a matter of pure physics. The formula for the generation of power is: power = force × velocity. In terms of racquetball, force is derived from a combination of torque and muscular contraction. The speed, or velocity, of the racquet is a product of the length of the swing, weight shift, the rapid extension of the elbow, and the whipping of the wrist at contact (Figure 7-1). Since the ultimate goal is to hit the ball with power, the objective of the stroke becomes to transfer maximum force to the racquet head while moving it at maximum speed. Maximum force and the ability to utilize it in the swing can be acquired through strength training.

Strengthening the Torque Center. Strength in the torque center is developed through resistance training. In all of the following exercises (Figures 7-2—7-8), overload is provided by the body parts, a

FIGURE 7-1 The hip and shoulder turn as elements of the total swing.

partner, or other types of external resistance. Each exercise should be performed with an amount of resistance that permits the completion of eight to fifteen repetitions. When fifteen repetitions can be performed using proper form, the resistance should be increased and the process repeated. For maximum results the exercises should be repeated every other day. These exercises were selected because they involve the muscles stressed in the racquetball stroke.

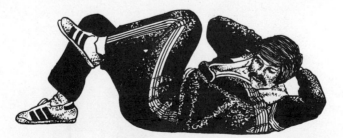

FIGURE 7-2 Strengthening the torque center. Start in a lying hook position with your hands behind your head. Perform a sit-up and twist and touch your right elbow to your left knee. Repeat on the opposite side.

FIGURE 7-3   (a) Back lying position with arms out to the side and legs perpendicular to the floor. (b) Slowly lower legs to one side, (c) getting as close to the floor as possible. Return to the starting position and repeat on the other side. Do not allow your arm and shoulder to rise off the floor as the legs are lowered.

FIGURE 7-4 Cross-legged sitting position with hands clenched in front of chest. Partner applies resistance at the elbow. Start with your shoulders rotated as far as possible in one direction. Rotate through the full range of motion against partner's resistance.

FIGURE 7-5 Stand with your feet shoulder-width apart. Hold a wand across your shoulders. Rotate your shoulders as far as possible in one direction. Partner applies resistance at the back of your opposite hand. Rotate against the resistance, attempting to move through the full range of motion.

FIGURE 7-6 (a) Straddle standing position holding a barbell with weight on one end and across the shoulders. (b) Bend to a ninety degree angle at your hips. Slowly twist your shoulders and move through a full range of motion against the resistance. Repeat with the weight on the opposite end of the barbell.

FIGURE 7-7 Standing erect, bend and grasp barbell. Legs should be slightly bent. Slowly move to a standing position as the weight is lifted to mid-thigh height. Lower the weight to the floor and repeat.

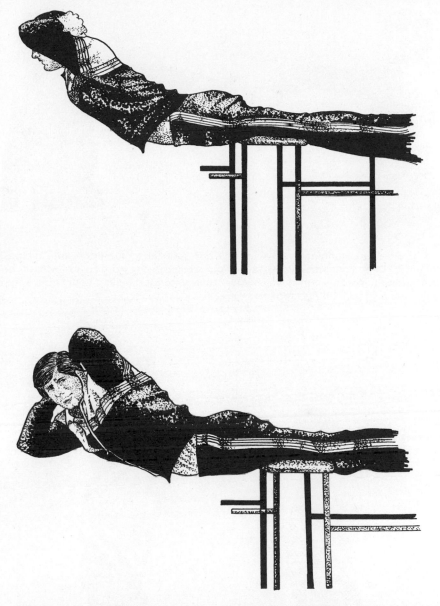

FIGURE 7-8 (a) Prone lying position with hands behind head. (b) Perform a back extension, lifting the head and shoulders as high as possible. Return to the prone position and repeat. *Variation:* While extending, rotate to one side by turning at the shoulders. Repeat on both sides.

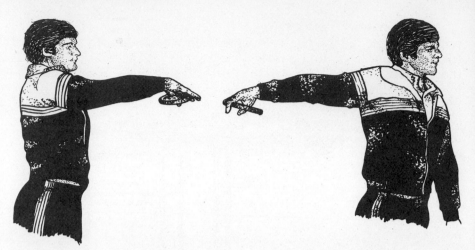

FIGURE 7-9 (a) Standing erect with one arm parallel to the floor and holding a weight. (b) Keep your arm parallel to the floor while moving from an arm-across-the-chest position to a position in which your arm is extended behind your body. Return to the starting position and repeat.

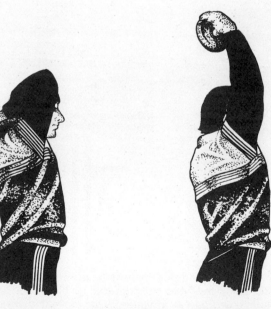

FIGURE 7-10 (a) Stand holding a weight with your arm bent and your elbow pointing toward the ceiling. (b) Your elbow must continue to point toward the ceiling as you straighten your arm. Return to the starting position and repeat.

Strengthening the Peripheral Component. In addition to strengthening the torque center, you should develop the muscles of the shoulder, elbow, and wrist to ensure maximal transfer of force to the racquet head. The following selected exercises should be performed according to the principles applied to the development of the torque center (Figures 7-9—7-12).

The game of racquetball has grown tremendously over the last ten years. Changes in equipment and training methods have converted the slow strategic approach of play to one of power. The player who hopes to compete at higher levels of play must develop overall fitness and the power component. Given equal basic skills, the player who is physically fit and who has worked on specific strength development will be the more consistent, powerful, and successful performer.

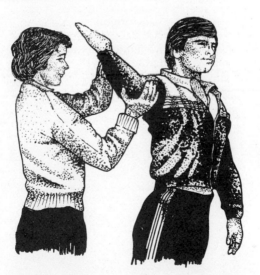

FIGURE 7-11 Stand with your elbow at shoulder height and bent at ninety degrees. Partner holds your elbow and gently pulls your shoulder into a position of full stretch. Resistance is then applied at your wrist as an attempt is made to rotate your shoulder through the range of motion. Return to the start and repeat.

FIGURE 7-12 Stand with your elbow at shoulder height and bent at a ninety degree angle. Partner holds your elbow and gently pulls your shoulder into a full stretch position. Resistance is applied to the back of your wrist and an attempt is made to move your shoulder through a full range of motion. Return to the start and repeat.

8

Officiating as an Art Form

The intent of this chapter is not to reproduce materials found in the rule book. It is to look at the mind-set and the demeanor needed to be a successful referee and to examine some of the situations that cause racquetball referees embarrassment and sleepless nights. Section 3, Rules 1A through 1G of the official rule book of the American Amateur Racquetball Association (AARA) (reprinted in Chapter 9) provides an excellent explanation of the responsibilities and duties of the three game officials. The complete set of rules for one-wall, three-wall, and eight and under "No Bounce" racquetball can also be found in Chapter 9. The true aficionado and the individual who hopes to play, teach, or referee the game should become well versed in the rules. The really good referees (in most players' minds there are no outstanding officials) are those who understand the rule book and know how to apply or interpret it during the changing situations of a game.

Most individuals who are called upon to referee in organized tournament play approach the task tentatively. This is understandable because (1) no one really teaches the majority of players how to referee, (2) most players are not that familiar with the rules, and (3) it appears to be an unpleasant job when one observes players having tantrums during play. Add to this the fact that the player who is asked to referee has just lost a match and plays at a level lower than that of the players in the upcoming match, and the lack of confidence and the total fright of the prospective referee is understandable.

The uneasiness experienced by the novice can be partly ameliorated if the role of the referee is understood and accepted. The primary function of the referee is to improve the quality of play. By properly interpreting the rules, the referee can stop one player from taking unfair advantage of another. When the referee is successful in fulfilling this task, the game flows more smoothly and the participants can compete safely.

Once you have accepted the basic concept of referring, the task becomes a mere matter of interpreting and applying the rules while maintaining your composure. The referee has to be the one "cool head" in chaotic and hotly contested matches. In many cases the players and spectators exhibit behaviors that can easily rattle the novice referee. Even the best referees get rattled at times, but there are certain personal characteristics they possess that protect them during the most difficult circumstances. The following characteristics can be cultivated by the aspiring referee and applied in game situations to take the RANKLE (irritations) out of the rigor of refereeing.

React Quickly and Make Immediate Calls.   The game is very fast paced and, of necessity, calls for split-second decision making on the part of the referee. There is no time for weighing the plusses and minuses in a given situation. If a correct call is not made when the infraction occurs, the actions that follow tend to confuse the situation and lead to arguments. The immediate correct call stops play at that point and focuses attention on the action that caused the infraction, eliminating the extenuating circumstances.

In several instances players who feel they have gotten a bad call can appeal. Players can appeal (1) a skipball, (2) a short serve, (3) a no-call on a serve felt to be short, (4) a double bounce that a player feels he or she received but the opponent did not get called on. In the case of an appeal, the referee asks for a second opinion. The linespeople are asked if they agree or disagree with the referee's call. If they agree, the call stands. If the linespeople disagree with the referee, the call is overruled, the correct one is made, and justice is served.

Players may not appeal hinders, avoidable hinders, and technical fouls. Quick, decisive calls in the case of hinders protects the players and eliminates subsequent play that could confuse the issue. Hinders and avoidable hinders are judgement calls and are the most difficult and controversial calls to make. However, if they are not made quickly and decisively, the referee can lose control of the match, and arguing and bickering can result.

The call which comes at the exact moment that an infraction occurs also helps the players gain a better understanding of the rule and possibly helps to eliminate players' mistakes and poor court positioning. The tactic of the player who backs into center court with eyes riveted on the front wall could be eliminated if referees would immediately call avoidable hinders. The player who loses several matches due to this maneuver is soon motivated to change such behavior.

Attend to the Game. There is nothing more disturbing to players and spectators than a referee who is not ready to start the match, does not know the score or which player is supposed to be serving, loses track of the number of time-outs taken, does not know which shot is being appealed, allows players to take extended time-outs and time between serves, and so on. These are the mechanical tasks of refereeing. No judgment is called for. You just have to be there and do your job to eliminate these problems. Players quickly lose confidence in the decision-making ability of the referee who is daydreaming or conversing with the spectators. The referee who pays attention to the menial tasks and watches closely during play finds it much easier to make the difficult calls, and his or her decisions are more readily accepted by the players.

Nonemotional Approach. The referee and the linespeople are usually geographically removed from the game by being placed in the viewers' gallery or behind a glass wall. It is much more difficult to remove these individuals from the action emotionally. Officials must be impartial observers and judges of the action. Players' personalities and intimidation should not become decisive factors in the decision-making process. The calls a referee makes should be the same in every like situation regardless of the individuals playing the game. If your best friend is playing, it is still a double bounce!

The referee must also be as calm as possible when conducting the game. In intense competitive situations calling for split-second decisions, disagreements are going to occur. Players will vociferously present their points of view, and it is the task of the referee to help them maintain their emotional control in these situations. The referee cannot afford to get involved in shouting matches with the players and spectators. This prolongs the event and focuses the discussion on things other than the decision at hand. In cases of disagreement, the referee should announce the decision, allow discussion at his or her discretion, let the player appeal the call if it is appealable, iterate the decision, and call for the serve. The server now has ten seconds to put the ball into play or it is a loss of serve. If the receiver continues to argue excessively, thereby delaying the serve, he or she can be given a "Referee's Technical." This results in a one-point deduction from the offender's score. The technical should be used sparingly; it is usually invoked when a player has lost all emotional control and is acting irrationally and immaturely. The situations calling for a technical foul are clearly spelled out in AARA Rules 14A through 14C. The referee who remains calm and emotionally detached from the action should be able to instill a quieting effect into the match.

Know the Rules.   A thorough knowledge of the rule book is essential to good play and refereeing. The procedures necessary to conduct and control a match are included in the rule book. A person who has no idea of how to play the game can conduct a match effectively and efficiently after having read and understood the rules. Thorough and accurate knowledge of the game can be gained by reading interpretations of the rules, questioning authorities, watching others play and referee and, most importantly, through experience. Take every available opportunity to referee. Refereeing practice games and tournament play helps hone your skills and increase your confidence. The majority of decisions made in a match are based upon direct *application* of the rules. The more difficult, or judgmental, decisions are made through *interpretation* of the fundamental rules. The referee who knows and can expound upon these rules can quickly end on-court arguments and gain the players' confidence.

Loud and Confident Announcements.   Most racquetball clubs have eight or more courts. During tournament or practice games, these courts are filled with players expressing their joy and sorrow and spectators reinforcing the participants' performances. In the midst of this environment stands the referee, twelve feet above the players and twenty feet away from the server. In order to be heard and to control the play you must be loud! This begins with the initial call of the score and continues throughout the match. A loud and clear "Zero serving Zero" brings the attention of the players, the spectators, and the linespeople to the action. A timid, low-volume pronouncement goes unheard and can result in player confusion, spectator noise, and inattentive linespeople. If this continues throughout the match, the flow of play and the concentration and quality of the participants' performance suffer.

Efficiently Conduct the Match.   It is the responsibility of the referee to run the match as quickly and effectively as possible. This means carrying out all of the prematch duties and being ready for play to begin on time. It is the responsibility of the players to be on the court and ready to play at the designated time. If a player or a team fails to report to play within ten minutes after the match has been announced, the match is forfeited. This appears to be a drastic measure, but it keeps the tournament on time, and it keeps one player from taking advantage of another. The player who is responsible and on time will be thoroughly warmed up and ready to play and will then have to wait until the opponent is ready. If the forfeit rule is not invoked, the more responsible player is at a disadvantage when play finally begins.

During a match, players often attempt to slow the game down for a variety of reasons. Players who are exhausted or are attempting to strategically slow the pace of the game stall between serves, continually call for a towel to wipe up wet spots on the floor and the ball, use more than their allotted thirty seconds during time-outs, use more than their allotted five minutes between games, feign injuries, and change their equipment frequently during the match. The efficient referee can quickly eliminate these tactics by following the guidelines spelled out in the rule book. When a player is stalling by walking around the court between serves, the referee can call the score shortly after the preceding rally has ended. The server and the receiver then have ten seconds to begin the next rally. If the ball is not put into play in ten seconds, it is a point or a side-out. In the case of the player delaying the game through cleaning the floor and extending the time-out and between-game periods, the referee can issue a technical foul and deduct one point from the offender's score. The injured player is allowed a total of fifteen minutes' rest during a three-game match, and if unable to continue, must forfeit. The referee who follows these guidelines can keep the match on time and stop one player from taking advantage of the other by violating the rules of the game.

If you play racquetball at any level, you are going to have to referee at some time. Even if you are only involved in a friendly game at the local club, the situation will arise when a discussion occurs and a decision has to be made. The person possessing the personal characteristics alluded to in this chapter will be able to effectively arrive at a solution acceptable to all. If you can do this without rankling your friends and opponents, you will raise the act of officiating to an art form.

9

The Rules of Racquetball

This chapter contains the complete set of rules for one-wall, three-wall, four-wall, and no-bounce racquetball. This section is reprinted with the permission of the American Amateur Racquetball Association. Inquiries concerning membership in the association or interpretations of the rules should be directed to the AARA (815 North Weber, Suite 203, Colorado Springs, Colorado 80903).

1982–84 AARA OFFICIAL RULE BOOK

THE GAME

A. Types of Games

Racquetball may be played by two, three, or four players. When played by two it is called "singles," when played by three, "cutthroat," and when played by four, "doubles."

B. Description

Racquetball, as the name implies, is a competitive game in which only one racquet is used by each player to serve and return the ball.

C. Objective

The objective is to win each rally by serving or returning the ball so the opponent is unable to keep the ball in play. A rally is over when a side makes an error, or is, unable to return the ball before it touches the floor twice, or if a hinder is called.

D. Points and Outs

Points are scored only by the server/(serving team) when it serves an ace or wins a rally. When the serving side loses a rally, it loses the serve. Losing the serve is called an "out" in singles, and a "hand-out" or "side-out" in doubles.

E. Game

A game is won by the side first scoring 21 points (or 11 points in the tie-breaker). A player need only win by one point.

F. Match

A match is won by the first side winning two games. The first two games of a match are played to 21 points, and the tie-breaker to 11 points. (Games may be won by one point.) In the event that each participant or team wins one game, the match shall be decided by an eleven (11) point tie-breaker.

G. Doubles Team

A doubles team shall consist of two players that meet either/or the age requirements or player classification requirements to participate in a particular division of play. A team must be classified by the ability level (or player classification) of the higher ranked player on the team.

A change in playing partners may not be made after the final draw has been made and posted. Under no circumstances can a partner change be made during the course of a tournament without the consent of the Tournament Director.

H. Consolation Matches

1. Consolation matches may be waived at the discretion of the tournament director, but this waiver must be in writing on the tournament application.
2. In all AARA sanctioned tournaments each entrant shall be entitled to participate in a minimum of two matches. This then means that losers of their first match shall have the opportunity to compete in a consolation bracket of their own division, in draws of less than seven (7) players, a round-robin format may be offered.

COURTS AND EQUIPMENT

A. Courts

The specifications for the standard four wall racquetball court are:

1. *Dimension.* The dimensions shall be 20 feet wide, 20 feet high, and 40 feet long, with a back wall at least 12 feet high. All surfaces within the court shall be deemed "in play" with the exception of any gallery openings or surfaces designated as "court hinders."
2. *Lines and Zones.* Racquetball courts shall be divided and marked with 1½ inch wide lines as follows:
   a. *Short Line.* The back edge of the short line is midway between (20′) and parallel to the front and back walls, thus dividing the court into equal front and back courts.
   b. *Service Line.* The front edge of the service line is parallel with and located five feet in front of the back edge of the short line.
   c. *Service Zone.* The service zone is the area between the outer edge of the short and service lines.
   d. *Service Boxes.* The services boxes are located at each end of the service zone and designated by lines parallel with each side wall. The inside edges of the lines are 18 inches from the side walls.
   e. *Receiving Lines.* Five feet back of the short line, vertical lines shall be marked on each side wall extending 3 to 6 inches from the floor. The back edge of the receiving lines shall be five feet from the back edge of the short line.

B. Ball Specifications

1. The standard racquetball shall be 2¼″ in diameter, weigh approximately 1.4 ounces, and at a temperature of 70–74°F., with a 100 inch drop rebound is to be 68–72 inches; hardness, 55–60 inches diameter.
2. Any ball which carries the endorsement stamp of approval from the AARA is an official ball. Only AARA approved balls may be used in AARA sanctioned tournaments.

C. Ball Selection

1. A ball shall be selected by referee for use in each match. During the match the referee either at his discretion, or at the request of a player or team, may replace the game ball. Balls that are not round or which bounce erratically shall not be used.

2. In tournament play, the referee and the players shall agree to an alternate ball, so that in the event of breakage, the second ball can be put into play immediately.

D. Racquet Specifications

1. *Dimensions.* The total sum of the length and width of the racquet may not exceed 27 inches. The length of the head, measured from the top of the handle to the top of the head, may not exceed 13.5 inches. The head width may not exceed 9 inches. These measurements are computed from the outer edge of the racquet head rims. The handle may not exceed 7 inches in length.
2. The regulation racquet frame may be of any material, as long as it conforms to the above specifications.
3. The regulation racquet must include a thong that must be securely attached to the player's wrist.
4. The string of the racquet should be gut, monofilament, nylon, graphite, plastic, metal, or a combination thereof, providing strings do not mark or deface the ball.

E. Uniform

1. The uniform and shoes may be of any color but must have soles which do not mark or damage the court floor. The shirt may contain any insignia or writing considered in good taste by the tournament director. Players are required to wear shirts. Extremely loose fitting or otherwise distracting garments are not permissible.
2. Eye protection is required for any participant under the age of 19 in *all* AARA sanctioned tournaments.

OFFICIATING AND PLAY REGULATIONS

Rule 1. A. Tournaments

All tournaments shall be managed by a committee or Tournament Director who shall designate the officials.

Rule 1. B. Officials

The official shall be a referee designated by the tournament director or the floor manager or one agreed to by both participants (teams in doubles). Officials may also include, at the discretion of the tournament director, a score-keeper and two linespeople.

Rule 1. C. Removal of Referee

A referee may be removed upon the agreement of both participants (teams in doubles) or at the discretion of the tournament director or rules officials. In the event that a referee's removal is requested by one player (team) and not agreed to by the other, the tournament director or officials may accept or reject the request.

Rule 1. D. Rule Briefing

Before all tournaments, all officials and players shall be briefed on rules and on court hinders or regulations or modifications the tournament director wishes to impose. This briefing should be reduced to writing. The current AARA rules will apply and be made available. Any modifications the tournament director wishes to impose must be stated on the entry form and in writing and be available to all players at registration.

Rule 1. E. Referees

1. *Pre-Match Duties.* Before each match begins, it shall be the duty of the referee to:
   a. Check on adequacy of preparation of court with respect to cleanliness, lighting, and temperature.
   b. Check on availability and suitability of materials necessary for the match such as balls, towels, score cards, pencils, and time piece.
   c. Instruct players on court.
   d. Point court hinders and local regulations.
   e. Inspect equipment and toss coin.
   f. Check linespeople and score keeper and ask for reserve game ball upon assuming officiating position.
   g. Review any rule modifications in effect for this particular tournament.
2. *Decisions.* During the match, the referee shall make all decisions with regard to the rules. Where linespeople are used, the referee shall announce all final judgments. If both players in singles and three out of four in a doubles match disagree with a judgment call made by the referee, the referee is overruled. The referee shall have jurisdiction over the spectators as well as players while the match is in progress.
3. *Protests.* Any decision not involving the judgment of the referee may, on protest, be decided by the tournament director or designated official.
4. *Forfeiture.* A match may be forfeited by the referee when:
   a. Any player refuses to abide by the referee's decision, or engages in unsportsmanlike conduct.
   b. A player or team may be forfeited by the tournament director or official for failure to comply with the tourna-

ment or host facility's rules while on the premises, for failure to referee, for improper conduct on the premises between matches, or for abuse of hospitality, locker room, or other rules and procedures.

c. Any player or team fails to report to play ten (10) minutes after the match has been called to play. (The tournament director may permit a longer delay if circumstances warrant such a decision.)

Rule 1. F.(1) Linespeople

Two linespeople are recommended for all matches from the semifinals on up, subject to availability and subject to the discretion of the tournament officials. The linespeople shall be selected by the officials and situated as designated by the officials. If any player objects to the selection of a linesperson before the match begins, all reasonable effort shall be made to find a replacement acceptable to the officials and players. If a player or team objects to a linesperson after the match begins, replacement shall be under the discretion of the referee and officials.

Rule 1.F.(2)

Linespeople are designated in order to help decide appealed rulings. Two linespeople will be designated by the referee and shall, at the referee's signal, either agree or disagree with the referee's ruling. The signal by a linesperson to show agreement with the referee is "thumb up." The signal to show disagreement is "thumb down." The signal for no opinion is "open palm down." If both linespeople signal no opinion, the referee's call stands. If both linespeople disagree with the referee, the referee must reverse the ruling. If one linesperson agrees and one disagrees or has no opinion, the referee's call shall stand. If one linesperson disagrees and one has no opinion, the rally or serve shall be replayed. Any replays will result in two serves with the exception of appeals on the second serve itself.

Rule 1. G. Appeals

In any match using linespeople a player or team may appeal only the following calls made (or failed to be made) by the referee:

1. Kill shots (skipballs); fault serves; out serves; double bounce pickups. The appeal must be directed to the referee, who will then request opinions simultaneously from the two linespeople. Any appeal made directly to a linesperson by a player or team or made after an excessive "demonstration" or complaint by the player(s) will be considered null and void and forfeit any appeal rights for that player or team for that particular rally.

2. *Kill Shot Appeals.* If the referee makes a call of "good" on a kill shot attempt which ends a particular rally, the loser of the rally may appeal

the call. If the appeal is successful and the referee's orieinal call reversed, the side which originally lost the rally is declared the winner of the rally. If the referee makes a call of "bad" or "skip" on a kill shot attempt, the rally has ended and the side against whom the call was made has the right to appeal the call if they felt the shot was good. If the appeal is successful and the referee's original call reversed, the referee must then decide if the shot could have been returned had play continued. If the shot could have been (or was) returned, the rally shall be replayed. If the shot was a kill or pass that the opponent could not have retrieved (in the referee's opinion), the side which originally lost the rally is declared the winner of the rally. The referee's judgment in this matter is final. Any rally replayed shall afford the server two serves.

3. *Fault Serve Appeals.* If the referee makes a call of "fault" on a serve, the server may appeal the call. If the appeal is successful, the server is entitled to replay the serve. If the served ball was considered by the referee to be an ace, then a point shall be awarded to the server. If the referee makes "no call" on a serve (therefore indicating that the serve was "good"), either side may appeal, then the situation reverts to the point of service with the call becoming fault. If it was a first service, one more serve is allowed. If the serve was a second serve, then the fault serve would cause an out.

4. *Out Serve Appeals.* If the referee makes a call of "out serve" thereby stopping the play, the serving side may appeal the call. If the appeal is successful, the referee shall revise the call to the proper call and the service shall be replayed or a point awarded if the resulting serve was an ace, if the referee makes "no call," or calls a "fault" serve, and the receiver feels it was an "out" serve, the receiver may appeal. If the appeal is successful the service results in an "out."

5. *Double Bounce Pickup Appeals.* If the referee makes a call of "two bounces," thereby stopping play, the side against whom the call was made has the right of appeal. If the appeal is upheld, the rally is replayed or the referee may award the rally to the hitter if the resulting shot could not have been retrieved by the opponent (and providing the referee's call did not cause the opponent to hesitate or stop play). If the referee makes "no call" on a particular play, indicating thereby that the player hit the ball before the second bounce, the opponent has the right to appeal at the end of the rally. However, since the ball is in play, the side wishing to appeal must clearly motion to the referee and linespeople by raising their non-racquet hand, thereby alerting the officials as to the exact shot which is being appealed. At the same time, the player appealing must continue to play. If the appealing player should lose the rally, and the appeal is upheld, the player who appealed then becomes the winner of the rally. All rallies replayed as the result of a double bounce pickup appeal shall result in the server getting two serves.

Rules Interpretations. If a player feels that the referee has interpreted the rules incorrectly, they may require the referee or tournament director to show them the applicable rule in the rule book.

Rule 2.   Serve

Rule 2. A.   Order

The player or side winning the toss becomes the first server and starts the first game. The loser of the toss will serve first in the second game. The player or team scoring the most total points in games one and two shall serve first in the tie-breaker. In the event that both players or team score an equal number of points in the first two games, another coin toss shall determine the server in the tie-breaker.

Rule 2. B. Start

The serve is started from any place within the service zone. No part of either foot may extend beyond either line of the service zone. Stepping on, but not over the line is permitted. The server must remain in the service zone from the moment the service motion begins until the served ball passes the short line. Violations are called "foot faults." The server may not start any service motion until the referee has called the score or second serve.

Rule 2. C. Manner

The serve is commenced by bouncing the ball to the floor while standing within the confines of the service zone and is struck by the server's racquet so that the ball hits the front wall first and on rebound hits the floor behind the back edge. of the short line, either with or without touching one of the sidewalls. A balk serve or fake swing at the ball shall be deemed an infraction and be judged an "out," "hand-out," or "side-out."

Rule 2. D. Readiness

Serves shall not be made until the receiving side is ready and the referee has called the score. The referee shall call the score as both server and receiver prepare to return to their respective position, shortly after the previous point has ended.

Rule 2. E. Delays

Delays on the part of the server or receiver exceeding 10 seconds shall result in an out or point against the offender.

1. This "10 second rule" is applicable to both server and receiver, each of whom is allowed up to 10 seconds after the score is called, to serve or be ready to receive. It is the server's responsibility to look and be certain that the receiver is ready. If the receiver is not ready, they must signal so by either raising their racquet above their head or completely turning their back to the server (these are the only two acceptable signals).
2. If the server serves the ball while the receiver is signaling "not ready," the serve shall go over with no penalty and the server shall be "warned" by the referee to check the receiver. If the server continues to serve without checking the receiver, the referee may award a "technical" for delay of game.
3. After the score is called, if the server looks at the receiver and the receiver is not signalling "not ready," the server may then serve. If the receiver attempts to signal "not ready" after that point, such signal shall not be acknowledged and the serve becomes legal.

Rule 3.   Serve in Doubles

Rule 3. A.   Server

At the beginning of each game in doubles, each side shall inform the referee of the order of service which shall be followed throughout the game. When the first server is out the first time up, the side is out. Thereafter, both players on each side shall serve until each receives a hand-out.

Rule 3. B. Partner's Position

On each serve the server's partner shall stand erect with back to the sidewall and with both feet on the floor within the service box from the moment the server begins his service motion until the served ball passes the short line. Violations are called "foot faults."

Rule 4.   Defective Serves

Defective serves are of three types resulting in penalties as follows:

Rule 4. A. Dead Ball Serve

A dead ball serve results in no penalty and the server is given another serve (without cancelling a prior illegal serve).

Rule 4. B. Fault Serve

Two (2) fault serves result in a handout.

Rule 4. C. Out Serve

An out serve results in a hand out.

Rule 5.   Dead Ball Serves

Dead ball serves do not cancel any previous illegal server. They occur when an otherwise legal serve:

Rule 5. A. Hits Partner

Hits the server's partner on the fly on the rebound from the front wall while the server's partner is in the service box. Any serve that touches the floor before hitting the partner in the box is short.

Rule 5. B. Screen Balls

Passes so close to the server or server's partner as to obstruct the view of the returning side. Any serve passing behind the server's partner and the side wall is an automatic screen.

Rule 5. C. Court Hinders

Hits any part of the court that under local rules is a dead ball.

Rule 5. D. Broken Ball

If the ball is determined to have broken on the serve, a new ball shall be substituted and the serve shall be replayed (not cancelling any prior fault serve).

Rule 6. Fault Serves

The following serves are faults and any two in succession result in an out.

Rule 6. A. Foot Faults

A foot fault results when:
1. The server does not begin the service motion with both feet in the service zone.
2. The server leaves the service zone before the served ball passes the short line.
3. In doubles, the server's partner is not in the service box with both feet on the floor and back to the wall from the time the server begins the service motion until the ball passes the short line.

Rule 6. B. Short Service

A short serve is any served ball that first hits the front wall and on the rebound hits the floor on or in front of the short line (with or without touching a sidewall).

Rule 6. C. Three-Wall Serve

Any served ball that first hits the front wall and on the rebound hits the two sidewalls on the fly.

Rule 6. D. Ceiling Serve

Any served ball that first hits the front wall and then touches the ceiling (with or without touching a sidewall).

Rule 6. E. Long Serve

Any served ball that first hits the front wall and rebounds to the back wall before touching the floor (with or without touching a sidewall).

Rule 6. F. Out of Court Serve

Any served ball that first hits the front wall and then goes out of the court.

Rule 7. Out Serves

Any of the following serves results in an out.

Rule 7. A. Failure of Server

Failure of server to put the ball into play within ten (10) seconds of the calling of the score by the referee.

Rule 7. B. Missed Ball

Any attempt to strike the ball that results in a total miss or in touching any part of the server's body other than the racquet.

Rule 7. C. Non-Front Serve

Any served ball that does not strike the front wall first.

Rule 7. D. Touched Serve

Any served ball that on the rebound from the front wall touches the server (or server's racquet) on a fly, or any ball intentionally stopped or caught by the server or server's partner.

Rule 7. E. Crotch Serve

If the served ball hits the crotch of the front wall and floor, front wall and sidewall, or front wall and ceiling, it is considered "no good" and is an out serve. A serve into the crotch of the back wall and the floor is good and in play. A served ball hitting the crotch of the sidewall and floor (as in a "Z" serve) beyond the short line is "good" and in play.

Rule 7. F. Illegal Hit

Any illegal hit (contacting the ball twice, carries, or hitting the ball with the handle of the racquet or part of the body or uniform) results in an out serve.

Rule 7. G. Fake or Balk Serve

Such a serve is defined as a non-continuous movement of the racquet towards the ball as the server drops the ball for the purpose of serving and results in an out serve.

Rule 7. H. Out-of-Order Serve

In doubles, when either partner serves out of order, any points which may have been scored during an out-of-order serve will be automatically void with the score reverting to the score prior to the out-of-order serve. The "out serve" shall be applied to the first server and the second server shall then be allowed to serve.

Rule 8. Return of Serve

Rule 8. A. Receiving Position

The receiver(s) must stand at least five (5) feet back of the short line as indicated by the vertical line on each sidewall, and cannot enter into this safety zone until the ball has been served and passes the short line. At that point the receiver(s) may enter the safety zone to return serve, however, neither the racquet nor body may infringe on the imaginary plane marked by the short line. A violation of the receiving zone or the short line by the receiver(s) results in a point for the server.

Rule 8. B. Defective Serve

The receiving side shall not catch or touch a defectively served ball until a call by the referee has been made or it has touched the floor for the second time.

Rule 8. C. Legal Return

After the ball is legally served one of the players on the receiving side must strike the ball with the racquet either on the fly or after the first bounce and before the ball touches the floor the second time to return the ball to the front wall, either directly or after touching one or both sidewalls, the back wall or the ceiling, or any combination of those surfaces. A returned ball may not touch the floor before touching the front wall.

Rule 8. D. Failure to Return

The failure to return a serve results in a point for the server.

Rule 9. Changes of Serve

Rule 9. A. Outs

A server is entitled to continue serving until:

1. *Out Serve.* The player commits an out serve as per Rule 7.
2. Player commits two fault serves in succession as per Rule 6.
3. *Hits Partner.* Player hits their partner with an attempted return.
4. *Return Failure.* Player or partner fails to hit the ball on one bounce or fails to return the ball to the front wall on a fly (with or without hitting any combination of walls and ceiling).
5. *Avoidable Hinder.* Player or partner commits an avoidable hinder as per rule 12.

Rule 9. B. Side Out

In singles, a single hand-out or out, equals a side-out and retires the server. In doubles a single hand-out equals a side-out on the first service of each game; thereafter, two hand-outs equal a side-out and thereby retire the serving team.

Rule 9. C. Effect

When the server, or the serving team receives a side-out, the server(s) become the receiver(s) and the receiver(s) become the server(s).

Rule 10. Rallies

Each legal return after the serve is called a rally. Play during rallies shall be according to the following rules:

Rule 10. A. Legal Hits

Only the head of the racquet may be used at any time to return the ball. The racquet may be held in one or both hands. Switching hands to hit a ball, touching the ball with any part of the body or uniform, or removing the wrist thong result in loss of the rally.

Rule 10. B. One Touch

In attempting returns, the ball may be touched or struck only once by a player or team or the result is a loss of rally. The ball may not be "carried." (A carried ball is one which rests on the racquet in such a way that the effect is more of a "sling" or "throw" than a hit.)

Rule 10. C. Failure to Return

Any of the following constitutes a failure to make a legal return during a rally:
1. The ball bounces on the floor more than once before being hit;
2. The ball does not reach the front wall on the fly;
3. The ball caroms off a player's racquet into a gallery or wall opening without first hitting the front wall;
4. A ball which obviously did not have the velocity or direction to hit the front wall strikes another player on the court;
5. A ball struck by one player on a team hits that player's partner, or a player is struck by a ball which was previously hit by that player, or partner.
6. An avoidable hinder as per rule 12 is committed.

Rule 10. D. Effect

Violations of Rule 10 A, B, and C result in a loss of rally. If the serving player or team loses the rally it is an "out" (hand-out or side-out). If the receiver(s) loses the rally, it results in a point for the server(s).

Rule 10. E. Return Attempts

1. In singles, if a player swings at, but misses the ball, the player may continue to attempt to return the ball until it touches the floor for the second time.

2. In doubles, if one player swings at, but misses the ball, both partners may make further attempts to return the ball until it touches the floor the second time. Both partners on a side are entitled to return the ball.

Rule 10. F. Out of Court Ball

1. *After Return.* Any ball returned to the front wall which on the rebound or on the first bounce goes into the gallery or through any opening in a sidewall shall be declared dead and the server shall receive two serves.
2. *No Return.* Any ball not returned to the front wall, but which caroms off a player's racquet into the gallery or into any opening in a sidewall either with or without touching the ceiling, side or back wall, shall be an out or point against the player(s) failing to make the return.

Rule 10. H. Broken Ball

If there is any suspicion that a ball has broken on the serve, or during a rally, play shall continue until the end of the rally. The referee or any player may request the ball be examined. If the referee decides the ball is broken, a new ball shall be put into play and the server given two serves. The only proper way to check for a broken ball is to squeeze it by hand. (Checking the ball by striking it with a racquet will not be considered a valid check and shall work to the disadvantage of the player or team which struck the ball after the rally.)

Rule 10. I. Play Stoppage

If a player loses a shoe or other equipment, or foreign objects enter the court, or any other outside interference occurs, the referee shall stop the play, if such occurrences interfere with ensuing play or player's safety.

Rule 10. J. Replays

Any rallies which are replayed for any reason without the awarding of a point or side-out shall result in any previous faults being cancelled and the server awarded two serves.

Rule 11. Dead Ball Hinders

Dead ball hinders result in the rally being replayed without penalty and the server receiving two serves.

Rule 11. A. Situations

1. *Court Hinders.* A ball that hits any part of the court which has been designated as a court hinder, or any ball that takes

an irregular bounce off a rough or irregular surface in such a manner as the referee determines that said irregular bounce affected the rally.

2. *Hitting Opponent.* Any returned ball that touches an opponent on the fly before it returns to the front wall. The player that has been hit or "nicked" by the ball may make this call, but it must be made immediately and acknowledged by the referee. Any ball which hits an opponent that obviously did not have the velocity or direction to reach the front wall shall not result in a hinder (and shall cause the player or team that hit the ball to lose the rally).

3. *Body Contact.* If body contact occurs which the referee believes was sufficient to stop the rally, either for the purpose of preventing injury by further contact or because the contact prevented a player from being able to make a reasonable return, the referee shall award a hinder. Body contact, particularly on the follow-through, is not necessarily a hinder.

4. *Screen Ball.* Any ball rebounding from the front wall close to the body of a player on the side which just returned the ball which interferes with or prevents the returning player or side from seeing the ball.

5. *Back Swing Hinder.* Any body contact either on the back swing or en route to or just prior to returning the ball which impairs the hitter's ability to take a reasonable swing. This call may be made by the player attempting to return if it is made immediately and it is subject to acceptance and approval of the referee.

6. *Safety Holdup.* Any player about to execute a return who believes they are likely to strike their opponent with the ball or racquet may immediately stop play and request a dead ball hinder. This call must be made immediately and is subject to acceptance and approval of the referee. (The referee will grant a dead ball hinder if he believes the holdup was reasonable and the player would have been able to return the shot, and the referee may also determine to call an avoidable hinder if warranted.)

7. *Other Interference.* Any other unintentional interference which prevents an opponent from having a fair chance to see or return the ball.

Rule 11. B. Effect

A call by the referee of a "hinder" stops the play and voids any situation following (such as the ball hitting a player). The only hinders a player may call are specified in Rules 11 A. 2, 11. A. 5, and 11

A. 6, and are subject to the acceptance of the referee. The effect of a dead ball hinder is that the player who served shall serve again, and shall be awarded two serves.

Rule 11. C. Avoidance

While making an attempt to return the ball, a player is entitled to a fair chance to see and return the ball. It is the responsibility of the side that has just served or returned the ball to move so the receiving side may go straight to the ball and have an unobstructed view of the ball after it leaves the front wall. In the judgment of the referee however, the receiver must make a reasonable effort to move towards the ball and have a reasonable chance to return the ball in order for a hinder to be called.

Rule 12. Avoidable Hinders

An avoidable hinder results in the loss of a rally. An avoidable hinder does not necessarily have to be an "intentional" act and is a result of any of the following:

Rule 12. A. Failure to Move

Does not move sufficiently to allow an opponent a shot.

Rule 12. B. Blocking

Moves into a position effecting a block on the opponent about to return the ball, or in doubles, one partner moves in front of an opponent as the partner of that opponent is returning the ball.

Rule 12. C. Moving into the Ball

Moves in the way and is struck by the ball just played by the opponent.

Rule 12. D. Pushing

Deliberately pushes or shoves opponent during a rally.

Rule 12. E.

Moves so as to restrict opponent's swing so that the player returning the ball does not have a free unimpeded swing.

Rule 12. F. Intentional Distractions

Deliberate shouting, stamping of feet, waving of racquet, or any manner of disrupting the player who is hitting the ball.

Rule 12. G. Wetting the Ball

The players, particularly the server, have the responsibility to see that the ball is kept dry at all times. Any wetting of the ball either deliberate or by accident, that is not corrected prior to the beginning of the rally shall result in an avoidable hinder.

Rule 13. Time-Outs

Rule 13. A. Rest Periods

During games to 21, each player or team is allowed up to three (3) thirty-second time-outs (2 per side in games to 11). Times-outs may not be called by either party after the server begins the service motion.

Rule 13. B. Injury

If a player is injured during the course of a match as a result of contact with the ball, racquet, opponent, wall, or floor they shall be granted an injury time-out. An injured player shall not be allowed more than a total of 15 minutes of rest during the match. If the injured player is not able to resume play after total rest of 15 minutes, the match shall be awarded to the opponent(s). Muscle cramps and pulls, fatigue, and other ailments that are not caused by direct contact on the court will not be considered an "injury."

Rule 13. C. Equipment Time-Outs

Players are expected to keep all clothing and equipment in good, playable condition and are expected to use regular time-outs and time between games for adjustment and replacement of equipment. If a player or team is out of time-outs and the referee determines that an equipment change or adjustment is necessary for fair and safe continuation of the match, the referee may award an equipment time-out not to exceed two minutes.

Rule 13. D. Between Games

A five minute rest period is allowed between all games of a match.

Rule 13. E. Postponed Games

Any games postponed by referees shall be resumed with the same score as when postponed.

Rule 14. Technicals

Rule 14. A. Technical Fouls

The referee is empowered to deduct one point from player's or team's score when in the referee's sole judgment, the player is being overtly and deliberately abusive. The actual invoking of this penalty is called a "referee's technical." If after the technical is called against the abusing player, and the play is not immediately continued, the referee is empowered to forfeit the match in favor of the abusing player's opponent(s). Some examples of actions which may result in technicals are:

1. Profanity. Profanity is an automatic technical and should be invoked by the referee whenever it occurs.
2. Excessive arguing.
3. Threat of any nature to opponent(s) or referee.
4. Excessive or hard striking of the ball between rallies.
5. Slamming of the racquet against walls or floors, slamming the door, or any action which might result in injury to the court or other player(s).
6. Delay of game, either in the form of taking too much time during time-outs and between games, in drying the court, in excessive questioning of the referee on the rules, or in excessive or unnecessary appeals.
7. Anything considered to be unsportsmanlike behavior.

Rule 14. B. Technical Warning

If a player's behavior is not so severe as to warrant a "referee's technical," a technical warning may be issued without point deduction.

Rule 14. C. Effect

If a referee issues a technical warning, it shall not result in a loss of rally or point and shall be accompanied by a brief explanation of the reason for the warning. If a referee issues a referee's technical, one point shall be removed from the offender's score. The awarding of the technical shall have no effect on service changes or side-outs. If the technical occurs either between games or when the offender has no points, the results will be that the offender's score will revert to a minus one (-1).

Rule 15. Professional

A professional shall be defined as any player (male, female, or junior) who has accepted prize money regardless of the amount in any PRO SANCTIONED tournament (WPRA, CATALINA) or any other association so deemed by the AARA Board of Directors.

1. A player may **participate** in a PRO SANCTIONED tournament which awards cash prizes, but will not be considered a professional if NO prize money is accepted.
2. The acceptance by a player of merchandise or travel expenses shall not be considered as prize money, and thus does not jeopardize a player's amateur status.

Rule 16. Return to Amateur Status

Any player who has been classified as a professional (see Rule 15) can recover amateur status by requesting, in writing, this desire to be reclassified as an amateur. This application shall be tendered to the Executive Director of the American Amateur Racquetball Association and shall become effective immediately as long as the player making application for reinstatement of amateur status has received NO money for the course of that year.

Rule 17. Age Group Divisions

Age is determined as of the first day of the tournament:

MEN'S AGE DIVISIONS:

Open—All players other than Pro
Junior Veterans Open—Amateurs 25 +
Veterans Open—Amateurs 30 +
Seniors—Amateurs 35 +
Veteran Seniors—Amateurs 40 +
Masters—Amateurs 45 +
Veteran Masters—Amateurs 50 +
Golden Masters—Amateurs 55 +
Senior Golden Masters—Amateurs 60 +
Veteran Golden Masters—Amateurs 65 +

WOMEN'S AGE DIVISIONS:

Open—All players other than Pro
Junior Veterans Open—Amateurs 25 +
Veterans Open—Amateurs 30 +
Seniors—Amateurs 35 +
Veteran Seniors—Amateurs 40 +
Masters—Amateurs 45 +
Veteran Masters—Amateurs 50 +
Golden Masters—Amateurs 55 +
Senior Golden Masters—Amateurs 60 +
Veteran Golden Masters—Amateurs 65 +

OTHER DIVISIONS

Mixed Doubles
Disabled

JUNIOR DIVISIONS

Age determined as of January 1st of each calendar year.

JUNIOR BOYS

18 years + under
16 years + under

JUNIOR GIRLS

18 years + under
16 years + under

14 years + under	14 years + under
12 years + under	12 years + under
10 years + under	10 years + under
8 years + under (no bounce)	8 years + under (no bounce)
Double Team—ages apply as above.	

Scoring—All matches in Junior Divisions will be the best of two games to 15 points, win by 1 point. If a tie breaker 3rd game is necessary the game is played to 15 points, win by 2 points up to 21 points, win by 1 point.

Junior Players should abide by all AARA rules with the following exceptions:

Rule 17. A. Eyeguards

Eyeguards *must* be worn in all AARA sanctioned events.

Rule 17. B. Time-Outs

Three in each game.

TOURNAMENTS

Rule 18. Draws

  a. If possible, all draws shall be made at least two (2) days before the tournament commences. The seeding method of drawing shall be approved by the American Amateur Racquetball Association.
  b. The draw and seeding committee shall be chaired by the AARA's Executive Director, National Commissioner, and the host Tournament Director. No other persons shall participate in the draw or seeding unless at the invitation of the draw and seeding committee.
  c. In local, state, and regional tournaments the draw shall be the responsibility of the tournament chairperson. In regional play the tournament chairperson should work in coordination with the AARA Regional Commissioner at the tournament.

Rule 19. Scheduling

  a. *Preliminary Matches.* If one or more contestants are entered in both singles and doubles, they may be required to play both singles and doubles on the same day or night with little rest between matches. This is a risk assumed on entering both singles and doubles events. If possible the schedule should provide at least one hour rest period between matches.

b. *Final Matches.* Where one or more players has reached the finals in both singles and doubles, it is recommended that the doubles match be played on the day preceding the singles. This would assure more rest between the final matches. If both final matches must be played on the same day or night, the following procedure is recommended:

1. The singles match be played first.
2. A rest period of not less than one (1) hour be allowed between the finals in singles and doubles.

Rule 20. Notice of Matches

After the first round of matches, it is the responsibility of each player to check the posted schedules to determine the time and place of each subsequent match. If any change is made in the schedule after posting, it shall be the duty of the committee or chairperson to notify the players of the change.

Rule 21. Third Place

Players are not required to play off for 3rd place or 4th place. However, for point standings, if one semifinalist wants to play off for third and the other semifinalist does not, the one willing to play shall be awarded third place. If both semifinalists do not wish to play off for 3rd and 4th positions, then the points shall be awarded evenly.

Rule 22. AARA Regional Tournaments

AARA Regional Tournaments—The United States and Europe are divided into a combined total of sixteen (16) regions.

a. A player may compete in only one regional tournament per year.
b. The defined area of eligibility for a person's region is that of their permanent residence. The only exception is when the locale of the adjoining regional tournament is closer to a player's residence than the site of their own home regional. In such a case the player is afforded the option of playing in either, but not both tournaments.
c. A player can participate in only two events in a regional tournament.
d. Awards and remuneration to the AARA National Championships will be posted on the entry blank.

Rule 23. Tournament Management

In all AARA sanctioned tournaments the tournament director and/or the National AARA official in attendance may decide on a change of courts after the completion of any tournament game if such a change will accommodate better spectator conditions.

Rule 24. Tournament Conduct

In all AARA sanctioned tournaments the referee is empowered to default a match if an individual player (or team) conducts themself (itself) to the detriment of the tournament and the game.

Rule 25. AARA Eligibility

Any paid-up AARA member in good standing, who has not been classified as a professional (see Rule 4.14), may compete in any AARA sanctioned tournament.

Rule 26. AARA National Championship

The National Singles and National Doubles were separated and will be played on different weekends. There will be a consolation round in all divisions.

> a. *Qualifying Singles.* A player may have to qualify at one of the sixteen (16) regional tournaments.

AARA Regions

> Region 1—Maine, New Hampshire, Vermont, Massachusetts, Rhode Island, Connecticut
> Region 2—New York, New Jersey
> Region 3—Pennsylvania, Maryland, Virginia, Delaware, District of Columbia
> Region 4—Florida, Georgia, North Carolina, South Carolina
> Region 5—Alabama, Mississippi, Tennessee
> Region 6—Arkansas, Kansas, Missouri, Oklahoma
> Region 7—Texas, Louisiana
> Region 8—Wisconsin, Iowa
> Region 9—West Virginia, Ohio, Michigan
> Region 10—Illinois, Indiana, Kentucky
> Region 11—North Dakota, South Dakota, Minnesota, Nebraska
> Region 12—Arizona, New Mexico, Utah, Colorado
> Region 13—Wyoming, Montana
> Region 14—Nevada, California, Hawaii
> Region 15—Washington, Idaho, Oregon, Alaska
> Region 16—Americans in Europe

1. The National Ratings Committee may handle the rating of

each region and determine how many players shall qualify from each regional tournament.

2. All National finalists in each division may be exempt from qualifying for the same division the following year.
3. There may be a tournament one day ahead of the National Tournament at the same site to qualify eight (8) players in each division who were unable to qualify or who failed to qualify in the Regionals.
4. This rule is in force only when a division is obviously oversubscribed.
   b. *Qualifying Doubles.* There will be no regional qualifying for doubles.

Rule 27. Intercollegiate Tournament

It will be conducted at a separate date and location.

ONE-WALL AND THREE-WALL RULES

Rule 28. One-Wall and Three-Wall Rules

Basically racquetball rules for one-wall, three-wall and four-wall are the same with the following exception:

One-Wall: Court Size—Wall shall be 20 ft. in width and 16 ft. high, floor 20 ft. in width and 34 ft. from the wall to the back edge of the long line. There should be a minimum of three (3) feet beyond the long line and six (6) feet outside each side line and behind the long line to permit movement area for the players.

Short Line—Back edge sixteen (16) feet from the wall.

Service Markers—Lines at least six (6) inches long parallel to and midway between the long and short lines, extending in from the side lines. The imaginary extension and joining of these lines indicates the service line. Lines are 1½ inches in width.

Service Zone—Floor area inside and including the short, side, and service lines.

Receiving Zone—Floor area in back of short line bounded by and including the long and side lines.

Three-Wall Serve—A serve that goes beyond the sidewalls on the fly, is considered "long." A serve that goes beyond the long line on a fly, but within the sidewalls, is the same as "short."

Court Size—short sidewall—20' in width and 20' in height and 20' in length. Sidewall shall extend back on either side from the front wall parallel 20' along the sidewall markers. Sidewall may extend from 20' at the front wall and taper down to 12' at the end of the sidewall. All other markings are the same as 4-wall.

*Court Size—long sidewall—*20' in width and 20' in height and 40' in length. Sidewall shall extend back on either side 40'. The sidewall may, but is not restricted to tapering from 20' of height at the front wall down to 12 feet at the 40' marker. All lines are the same as in 4-wall racquetball.

RULES FOR 8 & UNDER NO BOUNCE

Use AARA Racquetball rules with these modifications:

After a legal serve, the ball may bounce as many times as the receiver wants until he (or she) swings once to return the ball to the front wall. (In other words, they get one swing at the ball to get it back!)

The ball may be hit after the serve or during a rally at any time, but *must* be hit *before* it crosses the *short line* on its way *back* to the front wall.

The receiver can hit the ball before it hits the back wall or may play it off the back wall but cannot cross the short line *after* the ball contacts the back wall.

The only exception to crossing the short line is if the ball is returned to the back wall from the front wall on the fly (without touching the floor) then the receiver may cross the short line and play the ball on the first bounce.

New additions are lines on the front wall (use tape) at 3 ft. and 1 ft. high. If the ball is hit below the 3 ft. and above the 1 ft. lines during a rally, it has to be returned *before* it bounces the third time. If the ball hits below the 1 ft. line during a rally, it must be played or returned to the front wall before it bounces twice as in regulation racquetball. This gives incentive to keeping the ball low.

Games are played best 2 out of three games to 11 points.

HOW TO REF WHEN THERE IS NO REF

Rule 1—Safety

SAFETY IS THE PRIMARY AND OVERRIDING RESPONSIBILITY OF EVERY PLAYER WHO ENTERS THE COURT. At *no time* should the physical safety of the participants be compromised. Players are entitled, AND EXPECTED to hold up their swing, WITHOUT PENALTY, any time they believe there might be a risk of physical contact. Any time a player says he held up to avoid contact, even it he was overcautious, he is entitled to a hinder (rally replayed without penalty).

Rule 2—Score

Since there is no ref, or scorekeeper, it is important to see that there is no misunderstanding in this area, so THE SERVER IS RE-QUIRED to announce both the server's and receiver's score before EVERY first serve.

Rule 3—During Rallies

During rallies, it is generally the *hitter's* responsibility to make the call—if there is a possibility of a skip ball, double-bounce, or illegal hit, play should continue until the *hitter* makes the call against himself. If the hitter does not make the call against himself and goes on to win the rally, and the player thought that one of the *hitter's* shots was not good, he may "appeal" to the hitter by pointing out which shot he thought was bad and request the hitter to recon-sider. If the hitter is sure of his call, AND the opponent is still sure the hitter is wrong, the rally is replayed. As a matter of etiquette, players are *expected* to make calls against themselves any time they are not sure. In other words, if a shot is very close as to whether or not it was a good kill or a skip ball, unless the hitter is *sure* the shot was good, he should call it a skip.

Rule 4—Service

a. *Fault Serves (Long, Short, Ceiling & 3-wall):* The *RE-CEIVER* has the primary responsibility to make these calls, and again, he should give the benefit of the doubt to his opponent whenever it is close. The receiver must make his call immediately, and not wait until he hits the ball and has the benefit of seeing how good a shot he can hit. IT IS NOT AN OPTION PLAY . . . the receiver does not have the right to play a short serve just because he thinks it's a setup.

b. *Screen Serves:* When there is no referee, a screen serve DOES NOT BECOME AN OPTION PLAY. When the re-ceiver believes his vision of the ball was sufficiently im-paired as to give the server too great an advantage on the serve, the receiver may hold up his swing and call a screen serve, or, if he still feels he can make a good shot at the ball, he can say nothing and continue playing. HE MAY NOT CALL A SCREEN AFTER HE ATTEMPTS TO HIT THE BALL. Further, the server may not call a screen under any circumstances . . . he must simply expect to have to play the rally until he hears a call from the receiv-er. (In doubles, unless the ball goes behind the back of the server's partner, no screens should be called.)

c. Foot faults, 10-second violations, receiving-line violations, service-zone infringement and other "technical"
calls really require a referee. HOWEVER, if either player
believes his opponent is abusing any of these rules, between rallies he should discuss it with his opponent to be
sure there is agreement on what the rule is, and to put
each other on notice that the rules should be followed.

Rule 5—Hinders

Generally, the hinder should work like the screen serve—as an
option play for the hindered party. *ONLY* the person going for the
shot can stop play by calling a hinder, and he must do so immediately—not wait until he has the benefit of seeing how good a shot he can
hit. If the hindered party believes he can make an effective return in
spite of some physical contact or screen that has occurred, he may
continue to play. HOWEVER, as safety is the overriding factor, EI-
THER PARTY may call a hinder if it is to prevent contact.

Rule 6—Avoidable Hinders

Since avoidable hinders are usually not intentional, they do occur even in the friendliest matches. When a player turns the wrong
way and gets in the way of his opponent's setup, there should be a
better way than saying, "I'm sorry" to make up for the mistake. Instead of saying "I'm sorry," the player who realizes he made such an
error should simply award the rally to his opponent. If a player feels
his opponent was guilty of an avoidable, and the player did not call it
on himself, the "offended" player should appeal to his opponent by
pointing out that he thought it was an avoidable. The player may
then call it on himself, or disagree, but the call can only be made on
yourself. Often, just pointing out what you think is an avoidable will
put the player on notice for future rallies and prevent recurrence.

Rule 7—Disputes

If either player, for any reason, desires to have a referee, it is
considered common courtesy for the other player to go along with the
request, and a referee suitable to both sides should be found. If there
is not a referee, and a question about a rule or rule interpretation
comes up, seek out the club pro or a more experienced player, then,
after the match, contact your local state racquetball association for
the answer.

Glossary

AARA American Amateur Racquetball Association, governing body for amateur racquetball.

Ace Point-scoring serve that is not touched by the receiver.

Age Group Divisions Men's and Women's Divisions: Open—all players other than pros

Veterans Open—amateurs 30+
Seniors—amateurs 35+
Veteran Seniors—amateurs 40+
Masters—amateurs 45+
Veteran Masters—amateurs 50+
Golden Masters—amateurs 55+
Senior Golden Masters—amateurs 60+
Veteran Golden Masters—amateurs 65+

Junior Division—age is determined as of January 1 each year:
18 years and under
16 years and under
14 years and under
10 years and under
Under 8 years—"No Bounce"

Appeal Process a player uses to question a referee's call.

Arc   Trajectory of the bounce of the ball.

Around-the-Wall-Ball   Defensive shot that hits three walls—a side-wall, then the front wall, then another sidewall—and bounces into the back-court area.

Avoidable Hinder   Intentional or *unintentional* interference with an opponent's shot. It results in loss of a serve or a point. One of the three types of hinders.

Backhand Stroke   Hitting the ball from the nondominant side of the body.

Back-Wall Shot   Hitting the ball directly into the back wall in an attempt to get it to rebound to the front wall for a legal return.

Backswing   One of the nine elements of the stroke. Bringing the racquet back into position to initiate the forward swing.

Balk Serve   Fake swing on the serve, used to deceive the opponent. An automatic side-out in amateur play.

Bell Rope   Named after the rope one pulls to make a bell sound. The act of pulling this rope from an overhead position is similar to the motion used in the initiation of the swing.

Blocking   Moving in front of an opponent, thereby preventing the opponent from seeing or hitting the ball.

Boast   Shot that hits one sidewall, travels across the court to hit the other sidewall, and then skims across the front wall.

Bye   Movement of the top-seeded players in a tournament to the next round without their having played a match.

Ceiling Ball   Defensive shot that hits the ceiling, hits the front wall, and bounces over the opponent into the backcourt.

Center-Court Position   The place on the court that is equidistant from all four corners.

Combination System   System of doubles play that utilizes elements of the side-by-side and the "I" formation.

Complementary Shots   Shots used in sequence. The first shot sets up the second and increases its probability of success.

Contact Point   One of the nine elements of the stroke. The exact place where the ball is hit.

Control Player   Individual who excels at hitting the ball accurately.

Court Areas

   Front court—the area from the front wall to the service line

   Middle or center court—the area from the service line to approximately the receiver's line.

Back court—the last ten to fifteen feet of the court

Court Hinder Artificial interference introduced by the structure of the court, usually caused by a faulty door or a blemished wall.

Cross-Court Pass Ball hit from one side of the court to the deep corner of the other side.

Crotch Shot Ball that simultaneously strikes any two playing surfaces.

Cutthroat Form of racquetball played by three people. A rotation system is used in which the server always plays against the other two players.

Dead-Ball Hinder Situation in which the ball is no longer in play. The point is replayed. One of the three types of hinders.

Default Term used when, for any reason, a participant does not play.

Defensive Shot Used when a player is out of position or would have difficulty hitting an offensive shot. The objective is to move the opponent out of the center-court position.

Die Term used when the ball slows down during play.

Doubles Racquetball game in which two players compete against two other players.

Down-the-Wall Pass Shot that travels very close to the sidewall on its way to the front wall and returns in the same direction.

Draw Pairings for competitive play.

Drive Shot High velocity shot that hits only the front wall.

Drop Shot Soft shot usually hit from the front-court area. The ball rebounds only a short distance off the front wall.

Equipment Implements and objects needed to play racquetball. Specifications are listed in the AARA official rule book.

Equipment Time Out If a player's equipment breaks during play, a charged time out can be taken.

Eyeguard Mandatory piece of safety equipment that must be worn over the eyes in tournament play.

Fault Infraction committed while serving.

Fly Kill Volleying the ball (hitting it before it bounces off the floor) and attempting to hit it so low on the front wall that it cannot be retrieved.

Focal Point One of the nine elements of the stroke. It is where the player should be looking while attempting to hit the ball.

Follow-through One of the nine elements of the stroke. Deceleration and completion of the stroke.

Foot Fault   Infraction committed during the serve. The server or the doubles partner steps out of the service zone prematurely.

Forehand Stroke   Shot taken on the dominant side of the body.

Free Zone   Imaginary, unassigned area in doubles from which either player can hit the ball.

Front Wall, Sidewall Pinch Shot   A kill shot.

Game   One third of a match, completed when one player or team reaches twenty-one points.

Get   Term describing the act of retrieving the ball during play.

Grip   One of the nine elements of the stroke. Describes the way the racquet should be held for the forehand or backhand stroke. Also the name given to the material covering the racquet handle.

Half-Volley   Hitting the ball shortly after it has bounced, sometimes referred to as "short hopping" the ball.

Hand-Out   Referee's call designating a loss of serve. Used more frequently in doubles play; in singles it is referred to as a *side out.*

Hinder   See avoidable and dead-ball hinders.

"I" Formation   Used in doubles. One player is responsible for covering the front court area, while the other covers the backcourt.

Illegal Serve   Actually a fault serve. Can be a short serve, a three-wall serve, a ceiling serve, a long serve, an out-of-court serve, or a foot fault.

Kill Shot   Offensive shot that hits so low on the front wall that the opponent cannot retrieve it. Sometimes called a roll-out.

Levels of Play   Qualitative division of players into following divisions: Open, A, B, C, and Novice.

Linesmen   People assigned to a match to help the referee on appealed calls.

Lob Serve   Soft high-trajectory serve that strikes a point three-quarters of the way up the front wall and travels deep into the backcourt, where it skims the sidewall and dies near the back wall. The half-lob serve hits about head high on the front wall, bounces shortly after passing the short line, and bounces again before it hits the back wall.

Long Serve   Serve that hits the front wall and travels directly to the back wall without first hitting the floor.

Match   Contest that is completed when one player or team wins the best of three games.

Mechanics of the Skill   The way in which a skill is performed.

Mental Practice   Thinking about how to perform a skill, developing a mental picture of an activity.

Mixed Doubles   Co-ed racquetball teams.

Novice   Beginning or unskilled player.

Offensive Shot   Shot designed to score a point or result in a side-out.

Open Racquet Face   Usually occurs when the ball is contacted at the rear of the swing. The racquet is behind the hand at contact, and the face of the racquet is pointing toward the sidewall.

Overhead Shot   Kill, pass, pinch, or ceiling ball shots contacted above shoulder height.

Passing Shot   Ball that is hit to the side of an opponent so that it cannot be easily retrieved.

Peak of the Bounce   The place where the ball reaches its highest point, just before it begins to drop.

Pinch Shot   Ball that hits the sidewall and then the front wall, or the front wall and then the sidewall, in the front court area.

Power Player   Individual who excels at hitting the ball hard and low.

Power Serve   Epitome of the drive serve. The ball hits the front wall at a low point and "screams" across the short line before taking its first bounce.

Proactive Inhibition.   Interference in learning when acquisition of one skill makes it more difficult to learn a second skill.

Rally   Each legal return after the serve.

Receiver   Person returning the serve.

Receiving Line   Line on the sidewall that is five feet away from the short service line.

Referee   Head official, who controls the match and is responsible for calling the game.

Rollout   A shot hit so low on the front wall that the opponent cannot retrieve it.

Screen Serve   Serve that passes the server in such a way that the ball cannot be seen by the receiver.

Service Box   Part of the court used in doubles. The designated rectangular area at the end of the service zone.

Service Line   The front line in the service area, fifteen feet from the front wall. Used in calling foot faults.

Service Zone   Area bounded by the service line, the short service line, and the sidewalls.

Setup   Situation during play in which the offensive player should get an easy shot and score a point.

Shoot the Ball A kill shot.

Shooter Person who attempts a kill shot.

Short Line Line in the back of the service zone that is in the exact center of the court. Used to call short serves.

Side-by-Side Formation used in doubles in which each partner covers one vertical half of the court.

Side-Out Referee's call for a loss of serve.

Singles Racquetball game for two competitors.

Skip Ball Shot that hits the floor before reaching the front wall.

Splat Shot driven into the sidewall that rebounds to the front wall with a tremendous amount of sideward spin.

Stance The way a player stands during the stroke. Referents to the stance include

Open Stance—player's hips are facing the front wall

Closed Stance—during the forehand or backhand stroke, the lead foot steps and points toward the wall the player is facing

Middle of the Stance—area in the center of the body that cover a distance from head to toe and is approximately six inches wide.

Front of the Stance—area that covers a distance from head to toe and has a width from the front of the middle of the stance to a few inches in front of the lead foot.

Back of the Stance—area from head to toe that begins at the back of the middle of the stance and ends about two inches behind the rear foot.

Straddle Ball Ball that passes between the legs of a player who has just returned a shot.

Task Style Method of instruction based upon participants' individually practicing a variety of drills that stress various components of an activity.

Three-Wall Serve Fault serve that hits the front wall and two other walls before it bounces.

Up and Back The "I" formation used in doubles.

Volley Hitting the ball before it bounces.

Winner Shot that cannot be returned.

Wrist Action One of the nine elements of the swing, the one that imparts power to the stroke.

"Z" Serve Serve that is directed to the front wall at a point close to the sidewall. It then strikes the sidewall, travels across the court, bounces as it passes the short line, and hits the other sidewall.

Bibliography

AMERICAN ALLIANCE OF HEALTH PHYSICAL EDUCATION RECREATION AND
DANCE. *NAGWS Guide: Badminton/Squash/Racquetball.* Rest-
on, Va., May 1982–May 1984.

BUNN, JOHN W. *The Art of Officiating Sports* (3rd ed.). Englewood
Cliffs, N.J.: Prentice-Hall, Inc., 1968.

DOWELL, LINUS, AND WILLIAM GRICE. *Racquetball.* Boston: Standard
Publishing, American Press, 1979.

GARFINKEL, CHARLES. *Racquetball for the Serious Player.* New York:
Atheneum Publishers, 1982.

———. *Racquetball the Easy Way.* New York: Atheneum Pub-
lishers/SMI 1978.

KEELEY, STEVE. *The Complete Book of Racquetball.* Northfield, Ill.:
DBI Books, Inc., 1976.

MOSSTON, MUSKA. *Teaching Physical Education.* Columbus, Ohio:
Charles E. Merrill Publishing Co., 1981.

STAFFORD, RANDY. *Racquetball: The Book for Everyone.* Memphis:
The Stafford Co., 1975.

THOMPSON, WILLIAM, AND RICHARD GLEGG. *Modern Sports Officiating.* Dubuque, Iowa: William C. Brown Company, Publishers,
1974.

VERNER, BILL, AND DEW SKOWRUP. *Racquetball.* Palo Alto, Calif.: Mayfield Publishing Company, 1977.

VOCKELL, ED, AND OTTIS CAMPBELL. *Developing Racquetball Skills.* Niles, Ill.: Hewitt Printing Co., 1975.

Index